The Bimbo Has Brains
And Other Freaky Facts

The Bimbo Has Brains
And Other Freaky Facts

Author
Cathy Burnham Martin

Quiet Thunder Publishing
Manchester, NH

www.QTPublishing.com

This title and more are also featured at
www.GoodLiving123.com

The Bimbo Has Brains
And Other Freaky Facts

Paperback edition: ISBN 978-1-939220-39-4
eBook edition: ISBN 978-1-939220-40-0
Audiobook edition: ISBN 978-0-9832136-6-6

Published and printed in the United States of America.

Library of Congress Control Number:
2016951276

DEDICATION

I humbly and lovingly dedicate *The Bimbo Has Brains* to my husband, Ron Martin… a.k.a. Sir Ronald and The Ronald. We are imperfect people who have been blessed with many perfect and treasured life experiences.

Thank you, Sir Ronald for always reminding me that I am the smartest woman you've ever known… despite those inevitable Bimbo moments… and for sharing bountiful laughter and love, plus all the craziness that helps make you exactly who you are.

ACKNOWLEDGEMENTS

I gratefully acknowledge all of the dear friends who've told me their tales of triumphs and tears. We now hope that sharing their stories, both the challenges and the successes, helps give <u>you</u> courage and the powerful awareness that you are not alone. My special thanks to everyone who shared thoughts, opinions, and input to help this book be the best it could be.

TABLE OF CONTENTS

FOREWORD

*Hope is the whisper in our soul
that tells us all will be well.*

Cathy Burnham Martin has always exuded a common-sense approach to Life, well-seasoned with an unwaveringly positive attitude and sense of humor. When I first learned she was writing this book, I found myself saying, "Of course!"

Throughout her career, she's been a tireless encourager, sharing insights and offering support to all of us who've needed it. Naturally, in writing about relationships, her friends and associates welcomed the opportunity to be forthcoming with their stories to help people weave their way through personally challenging times.

Her informal writing style feels as if she's talking directly with the reader. She writes from her heart and speaks to our hearts. I've never known her to be any other way.

Upon hearing my thoughts on "The Bimbo Has Brains," she immediately began encouraging me to write a companion book, "The Golf Pro Has Heart." Her confidence never waned that my wisdom and experiences needed to be shared.

Cathy knew our different perspectives would reign far above the "he said, she said" realm. She is right.

She does more than claim the positive. She lives it and teaches everyone around her to capture their magic, too. She is no Bimbo. Then again, as she says, we all have our Bimbo moments. Cathy Burnham Martin also has Brainiac moments. I've been a fan, but I am most proud to say she is my friend.

John A. Gehrisch

ABOUT JOHN A. GEHRISCH

Not every electrical engineer can parlay a successful sales and marketing career into the professional golf circuit. But John Gehrisch is far from typical. President of BBJM Golf Ventures, the exclusive golf memorabilia producer since 2003, John has enjoyed golf since he got out of college. It was his Dad who dreamed of John becoming a golf tour professional.

That was after founding and running a successful wire and cable insulating company, PMC Corporation, which, prior to its sale, produced enough wire in one year to wrap around the world 13 times. It's no wonder that financial guru Warren Buffet chose to purchase PMC Corporation. This enabled Gehrisch to direct successful turnarounds for struggling companies. He was honored to serve on the New Hampshire Governors Round Table and the U.S. Presidential Round Table.

Golf remained his passion. As soon as he turned pro in 1999, he started playing on the mini tours, finishing second several times prior to winning his first event on the Western States Tour in early 2000. He has played on and off on the Senior PGA Tour (now the Champions Tour) and been paid to compete in international professional tournaments as far away as the Azores and Morocco.

OTHER TITLES
From Cathy Burnham Martin

A Dangerous Book for Dogs: Train Your Humans

Dog Days in the Life of the Miles-Mannered Man

Healthy Thinking Habits: Seven Attitude Skills Simplified

Of the Same Blood: Your Eurasian Heritage

Sage, Thyme & Other Life Seasonings: Perspectives

Fifty Years of Fabulous Family Favorites, Volumes 1-3

Champagne! Facts, Fizz, Food & Fun

Boat Drinks

Dockside Dining: Round One

Dockside Dining: A Second Helping

Dockside Dining: Back for Thirds

Cranberry Cooking

Lobacious Lobster

The Communication Coach:
Business Communication Tips from the Pros

**To see all books and audiobooks from Cathy Burnham Martin
go to www.GoodLiving123.com**

PREFACE

Why This? Why Now? Say What?!!?

During a brief marriage to a disturbingly misogynistic man, I began to lose myself. What had started out as a seemingly supportive and loving rebound-relationship had rapidly turned frightening, controlling, and extraordinarily dangerous. Demeaning behavior became "the norm," rather than the exception.

One evening, as I washed the dinner dishes, unable to hold back my silent tears of despair, deliberately thrown knives whizzed repeatedly past my face into the wall amidst the increasingly usual barrage of disparaging insults and swears also hurled my way. I started to believe I could not get out of that marriage alive.

When a gun was waved in my face and a knife pressed to my throat, I did not think I would even make it through the night.

Thankfully, most people cannot imagine such an existence. The person you love morphs into the person you most fear. Though they espouse their deepest love for you, you start to recognize that the emotions your partner expresses do not even distantly resemble love. You become unsure they actually *can* love.

However, you also become certain that you can never escape their tangled web. I knew that I would remain in his crosshairs until such time as he believed he was in love with someone else.

I prayed… a lot. Sadly, one of my prayers was that God would just "take" him in his sleep. I did not wish him pain, or fear, or harm, but I did not often believe I could escape with my own life.

I thank God to this day for blessing me with a tremendous network of strong, loving family, friends, and co-workers. They hid me, helped me, and loved me through the darkest time in my life.

Though it took me several years, I emerged a better person. I look at life differently. I breathe the air more gratefully. I believe more profoundly.

Finally, a few years after that marriage, I even dared to date again, although the "ex" had sneered that no one would ever want such "damaged goods." No problem.

Okay, to be honest, I guess I was never very good at dating. I had many "men friends," but truly dating someone for me was rare. I busied myself with work, family, faith, and community. My life felt full. For some of us, including me, the journey to a happy and stable relationship has been far from smooth.

I continued to question everything, especially my unpredictably uncontrollable need to apologize for seemingly everything, including things fully out of my control.

What had led me to my deadly downward spiral in the first place? How did my self-confidence shatter so dramatically? Is it even fathomable that a highly intelligent, successful woman could be emotionally and psychologically squashed like a bug?

I was working in television news at the time. Dread filled my heart and my blood ran cold on more than one occasion when my then estranged husband would suddenly appear out of the dark, as I walked with a security guard from work to my car, or as I left a location where a videographer and I had been covering a story.

This was before stalking laws "got teeth," so a physical and psychological cat-and-mouse game often seemed unavoidable. I drove a long series of rent-a-wreck cars. I let co-workers disguise me in various hats and coats to sneak me out of work. I lived, cowered in a basement, with all windows completely covered.

I feared for my safety and that of everyone around me…family, friends, and co-workers… because he repeatedly made it very clear that I should.

Like the veritable circus clown, I struggled to keep my head held high with a smile on my face, while tears and terror flowed within me... *every* day for several years. I continued to move through my surreal world, putting one foot in front of the other, never sure what lurked around the next corner.

The vast majority of people had absolutely no idea.

Later, I produced and hosted an important documentary on intimate partner abuse. "Domestic Violence: When Home Is No Haven" revealed the truth and terror for women and men who are victimized by their partners. Throughout the entire making of the program, I continually repeated to myself, "There, but for the Grace of God, go I."

Sometimes, especially after surviving horrendous terror and heartbreak, personal pain and disturbing discouragement, we just want to curl up and hide from the world. Perhaps I was most fortunate to be working in a very public and visible career. I could not hide nor quietly slip through my days unnoticed.

Instead, I had to work through my trauma in full view of a close-up camera. I chose to practice the old, "Fake it till you make it" thinking. I needed to learn and grow. I had to survive to thrive. The confusion, exhaustion, and constant stress aged me rapidly.

For me, life has since taken many delightful turns. Thanks to my strong faith and the friendship and love of the many wonderful people who are currently in and who have passed through my life, I was able to turn my sadness and shame into energy and enthusiasm for helping others do and live better. Emerging from that darkest personal chaos is likely the core reason I now write for the **www.GoodLiving123.com** blog, where I can share information with people who'd like help making good living as easy as 1-2-3.

No matter the circumstances, when you've survived an unhealthy relationship, the pain, uncertainty, and fear never really leave you. They always remain, ever bubbling just below the surface.

That probably has helped me relate to a wide variety of people with sincerity, empathy, and compassion, and even to encourage others to blossom. I never set out to become someone people repeatedly call "The Morale Booster," but it has been my humble honor to try to live up to their confidence in me.

Despite a number of previous books, including some with personal tales and tidbits, I only now decided to openly admit the false existence and core unhappiness that I kept hidden so well.

There. I have done it. Enough said.

"The Bimbo Has Brains… and Other Freaky Facts" is not about me nor my sordid personal journey, although those experiences most assuredly developed my awareness of so many of life's facets.

This book *is* about many of the perception and relationship realities we *all* share and endure in our search for happiness. My concepts evolved from observing, experiencing, and learning from others, as we find our way and develop perspective.

Each of us is on a different, yet intrinsically-shared journey.

Now, thanks to my growth, I can not only help others find their way through this fascinatingly varied maze we call Life, but I can offer both humor and hope. Join me now, as we shed light, learning, and laughter on loving relationship scenarios and foibles that can sometimes seem highly confusing.

Who knows? I just may even encourage other "darkness" survivors to step out "into the Life."

Author's Note: If you would like valuable information and statistics on the domestic violence reality in the U.S.A., please refer to this book's Afterword, which also includes resources.

Section 1

OPEN THE DOOR

1
<u>Setting the Stage</u>

Since light travels faster than sound,
people may appear bright until we hear them speak.

Years ago someone asked me what the title of a book about me would be. It was just one of those goofy "stump-the-student" questions. You've got to love those.

- "If you were an animal, what would you be?"
- "If you were naming yourself, what name would you choose?"
- "If you ran away and joined the circus, what job would you want?"

The list goes on and on. Management gurus tell you that your answers to such questions parallel various personality traits and behavior patterns.

I'd make them crazy. I'd be the clown who tames the lions, while performing on the flying trapeze, munching popcorn, and welcoming the ladies and gentlemen and children of all ages to the greatest show on earth.

All that really means is that I don't know what I want to be when I grow up. (Not that I actually have plans to grow up.) It also means that I try to "do it all," resulting in my knack for being a "Jack-of-All-Trades, Master-of-None."

Meanwhile, all this living makes me smile. We humans tend to have so many firm, preconceived notions. We try to put other people in highly-defined boxes, and they do the same with us. Naturally, we never quite think of ourselves as possibly fitting so neatly into some easily definable box.

Anyway, after collecting a few decades' worth of chuckles over my "expected Bimbohood," I found the answer to the book title question.

It actually came to me during a Miss America-related pageant experience. While talking with two men, they quipped about what a "bunch of bimbos" the young women were.

I reminded them of the irony. These "bimbos" get asked questions about building world peace, solving global economic woes, curing racial divides, saving the planet, and many other topics that stump top world leaders. I concluded with, "Brace yourselves. These Bimbos have brains."

So, again, though not "my story," this book reveals a lot of what I've learned about our human experience, especially surviving and thriving in relationships, both from my own experiences and those of many others.

As tempting as it may be to serve up a juicy "tell-all" relationship book, I believe the only purpose *that* serves is to perpetuate the already raucous battle of the sexes. This is somber stuff that needs to be looked at with far more than a healthy grain of genuine humor… and compassion.

Remember, humor isn't always funny. But Life is often laughable, even when marked with pathos. We take ourselves so seriously it can be maddening.

If you've seen Jimmy Buffett in concert, you may well recall his "Fruitcakes" song. At one point, he says, "Now here comes the big one… relationships. We all *got* 'em. We all *want* 'em. What do we *do* with 'em?"

Well, we struggle. We flourish. We love, and we ache. We rant, and we rave. We hurt, and we *get* hurt. We lie. We cheat. We survive. We thrive. We forgive… and we move on.

We are, after all, merely humans, with mountains of issues, vulnerabilities, and dreams. Through all the highs and lows, it sure helps to have a healthy self-image, sense of humor, and faith.

It matters not how many "bimbo moments" you may have. We all do. Anyone who claims *not* to have brain cramps now and then lies about other things, too. Guaranteed.

So, here we go… dealing with twists and turns that may have thrilled, tempted, or even tortured your soul.

Relax. You are not alone.

We'll laugh… and snarl… together.

From the outset, let's recognize that, of course, not every woman is a bimbo, despite earnest media attempts to make us think that we should at least try to *look* like one. That said, it's equally important to understand that not all men are cavemen. Some are even bimbos.

However, the best of us, both men and women, do have more than a few things in common. These include such treasures as some fine brain power, a solid sense of humor, and a healthy dose of confidence tempered with humility.

Enjoy the facts, fiction, and fun on the next pages. No matter what the colloquialism of the day may be, more than a few times you just may find yourself saying, "Duh," "Really?" or "Oh, yeah!"

A good number of friends have shared from their hearts and souls, so as to give you perspectives and considerations that you may or may not have previously pondered.

Many names, places, and dates have been changed to protect the guilty… and the innocent. ☺

"The Bimbo Has Brains" unleashes a wide variety of their observations from personal experiences, ongoing and foiled relationships, successes and failures, smooth moves and faux pas. These true stories and heart-felt scenarios may help you feel connected and not alone in some experience of your own.

Also, references to him or her, men or women, husbands and wives, male and female, can frequently be reversed. A wife may share a story that you recognize in your own life, only it happened to the husband. I am not at all certain that most experiences or thoughts or approaches are more specific to men or to women.

That said, there are definitely some "he said / she said" items in here. And I admit that my own experience and mere humanness land me squarely on the "she said" side of most conversations.

If something is discussed as common or typical, it simply means it is common or typical. It should not to be misconstrued as meaning "always" or "stereotypically."

Both men and women are guilty and innocent of many of the same things.

Relationship topics range from stereotyping, stress, and aging to dealing with lies, cheating, and forgiveness. In Volume 2, "The Bimbo Has *More* Brains," we delve into political "quackiness," the New American Revolution, money, media mayhem, and much more that stretches through and beyond personal relationships.

Nothing is off limits with "The Bimbo Has Brains," including men versus women, feelings versus logic, and being sensual versus sexual. Observations, secrets, opinions, and shared gems of wisdom have been gleaned over many years of heartache and joy.

Tip: When you find time-tested and experience-proven shortcuts, take them. Save yourself time, heartache, and grief.

2
<u>What Is a Bimbo?</u>

The IQ test showed she was extremely beautiful.

I care little if my lingo lacks political correctness. Or, as I call it, "political quackiness." We all need to lighten up. If we can't laugh at ourselves, we become pretty tough to take seriously. Seriously.

A standard dictionary defines "bimbo" as an attractive, but empty-headed young woman, especially one perceived as a willing sex object. A bimbo is considered foolish, stupid, and inept, by any definition.

The online Urban Dictionary says it's a girl who is stupid, wears lots of make-up and is obsessed with boys and clothes. It also defines a bimbo as generally blonde, though there are exceptions. The definition further notes that, they "usually hang around with other bimbos, and you can spot them because they will be the big group of girls that all look the same and are giggling hysterically."

The Mirriam-Webster Dictionary acknowledges that a bimbo is a disapproving term for an attractive, but vacuous man or woman.

American "slanguage" landed "bimbo" squarely in our minds as a female, brain-free zone, most often the stereotypical "dumb blonde." If referring to a male, a couple of other terms evolved, including "himbo" and "mimbo."

From my perspective, I hear people who've forgotten something saying they'd had a "brain cramp" or a "senior moment." Well, I like flying in the face of sensibilities, laughing at myself before anyone else gets the chance. I simply say that I am having a "bimbo moment."

I apply the same to male friends who've just said something silly or who've been forgetful, acknowledging that they also have "bimbo moments."

We should all feel free enough to make both smart and silly comments… to remember and to forget… to break out of any box or limitations that society or anyone tries to set for us. Sometimes very smart people come across with bimbo statements.

None of us should claim to have never gotten our "mords wixed." (Er… Uh… words mixed.) We need to be able to laugh at ourselves and be less judgmental of both ourselves and others.

In May, 2008, while campaigning in Oregon, then Presidential nominee, Barack Obama, said he'd already visited 57 of our states, with just one more to go. "I've now been in 57 states, I think. One left to go. Alaska and Hawaii… "

I don't care where you stand politically, this is a smart man who got his "mords wixed."

Some celebrities seem to love fueling an image of being none-too-smart. They wear dopiness as if it was a badge of excellence.

American socialite Paris Hilton comes to mind. It's hard to forget her alleged comments about having travelled to London, but never to England. Or her supposed wonderments about whether or not Wal-Mart was a store that sells walls. Okayyy. No one actually takes what she says seriously, other than perhaps Hilton herself.

Far too many celeb types work hard to be or at least come off as dopey. Early 21st Century pop culture is rife with the likes of "reality TV" personality Kim Kardashian, social media personality Tila Tequila, British-American actress Mischa Barton, Canadian-American actress Pamela Anderson, "reality TV" personality Heidi Montag, and singer Jessica Simpson.

Whether accurate or not, various celebrities have been quoted and misquoted with a wide range of bimbo comments. The media loves faux pas.

For example, when model Brooke Shields says something meaningful and serious, it doesn't get air time. But fasten your seatbelt. Shields is reported as having said, "Smoking kills. And if you're killed, you've lost a very important part of your life." Hmmm. Of course, accurate or not, *that* gets ink… airtime… a gazillion hits on the Internet.

Jessica Simpson allegedly claimed, "I'm not anorexic. I'm from Texas. Are there people from Texas that are anorexic? I've never heard of one. And that includes me." Ummm… I don't even know where to begin on that one.

Television actress Tara Reid supposedly said, "I make Jessica Simpson look like a rock scientist." There's no typo there. She said "rock scientist," not "rocket scientist."

Former Czech-American model and ex-wife of Donald Trump, Ivana Trump is reported as having stated, "Fiction writing is great. You can make up almost anything." Yes, indeed.

Singer Christina Aguilera is said to have once asked, "So, where is the Cannes Film Festival being held this year?" Wait. I know! I know! Same place as last year.

Former Hilton gal-pal Nicole Richie is often noted for displaying her firm grasp on reality. "When I pictured heroin, I pictured some crazy crack head with no shoes under a bridge. You never think that is going to be you. And it never was me. I was never under a bridge, and I always had shoes." Okayyy.

Now, there are also plenty of male celebrities who embrace "bimbohood." They are also stereotyped as more attractive than smart.

What Is a Bimbo?

Descriptive words range from mindless meatheads and gum-smacking beef cakes to phrases like boy toys and hollow-headed bimbos with balls.

They may be dim as donuts, but plenty of guys have earned a living on their looks, whether or not they were actually very intelligent. Consider actor and dancer Patrick Swayze, television star David Hasselhoff, "reality TV" personality Spencer Pratt, and film star Keanu Reeves, just for starters.

David Hasselhoff is alleged to have claimed, "I've got taste. It's inbred in me." Oh, please. He couldn't possibly have meant that.

Body builder, movie star, and former California Governor Arnold Schwarzenegger may have commented, "I think gay marriage is something that should be between a man and a woman." Terminate those "wixed mords."

Soccer star David Beckham showed his religious savvy when he allegedly said, "I definitely want Brooklyn to be christened, but I don't know into what religion yet." David, check the word Christ in "christened" for a hint. Amen.

Numerous characters in movies and television series delightfully wormed their way into the hearts of audiences with their foolishness. Consider dim characters like Joey Tribbiani on "Friends" or Joey Russo on "Blossom." The characters may lack personality, but cute hunks seem to sell... very well.

When actors portray smart characters who don't appear smart on the surface, we find some great stories and comedy. Take the Elle Woods character in "Legally Blonde," for example. She was highly intelligent, but caught people off guard with her "cutesy" appearance and mannerisms. The movie's success sparked a sequel and a Broadway musical.

There's also the famous Marilyn Monroe character, Lorelei Lee, in "Gentlemen Prefer Blondes." Sexy and sassy, perfectly played as only a smart actress could.

Like it or not, when someone calls someone a Bimbo in this day in age, they are typically referring to a woman… a woman they consider non-thinking. So much has been said by and about women, the ditzy rantings have become cliché.

But we should all be okay with having bimbo moments. We all do have them. We need not be blonde, or glamorous, or famous, or female. We don't even need to be "all flash and no substance." We just have to be human.

Tip:

*"I hate to hear you talk about all women as if they were
fine ladies instead of rational creatures.
None of us want to be in calm waters all our lives."*
                                                            - Jane Austen (1775 – 1817)
                                                            English novelist

3
Historically Speaking

I've made the same mistakes so many times
I now call them traditions.

Let's look at the word "bimbo." It originates from the Italian word bimbo, meaning a baby boy or young male child. By the beginning of the 20th Century, bimbo had entered the American language, but its meaning referred to an unintelligent or brutish man. By the 1920's, the term began to include and even shift to women, especially those perceived to be of questionable virtue.

Maybe we shouldn't fret about being a bimbo or a himbo. Saying himbo after bimbo is actually redundant, since bimbo's true meaning is male.

But even in recent history, the word bimbo has been flung around with great disdain in its meaning.

In August, 2015, Time Magazine reported on how former Hewlett-Packard CEO and 2016 Republican Presidential candidate, Carly Fiorina, said that she'd "been called a bimbo at work." Obviously, she is no bimbo by any traditional nor urban definition standards.

A feud sparked in January, 2016, when people tweeted about Fox News' Megyn Kelly, calling her a bimbo for a sexy 2010 photo shoot in "GQ" magazine. Then Republican Presidential candidate, Donald Trump, caught tons of Internet flack for retweeting the pictures of Kelly and questioning if this was "the bimbo asking presidential questions."

Perhaps Mr. Trump found it rather twisted that someone supporting the objectification of women by posing for such a photo shoot would be a presidential debate moderator whose first question to him regarded his language objectifying women. Point taken.

Regardless, name calling is just plain bad. It would seem that Kelly didn't think through her 2010 image choice any more than Trump thought through his bimbo comments. Both sought serious professional credibility. Both goofed up in the bimbo arena, but Kelly wasn't running for President.

Not to provide an excuse for Trump, by any means, but a precedence for treating women in a disgusting manner had been set in White House politics long before Donald Trump ran for President and became the unwitting leader of what I dubbed the New American Revolution. His reportedly sexist attitude had little bearing on the American people's recognition of our nation's urgent need for new leadership. Throughout the Presidential Primary, people stood up en masse and rejected the political machine of the Republican Party.

Donald Trump did not need to be a perfect person. No one expected that. In fact, it may have been seen as refreshing to have foibles and faux pas exposed. It turned out to make the business tycoon and media mogul more genuine.

One big difference surfaced regarding sexism. In the 2016 Presidential race, the population knew up front what previously had only been revealed later.

For example, the many sexual escapades of President John F. Kennedy have surfaced and become legendary. Fans of more recent U.S. Presidential politics may recall Hillary Clinton's 1990's "war room" against what she called the "Bimbo Eruptions" throughout Bill Clinton's political campaigns and presidency.

Clinton's numerous exploits include a multi-year affair with Arkansas TV reporter Gennifer Flowers.

At least four other women went on the record accusing him of sexual harassment to rape. They include Kathleen Willey, Juanita Broaddrick, Eileen Wellstone and Paula Jones. Willey has also accused Hillary Clinton of using mob-like tactics to intimidate her into silence.

A long list of people cite tales of *his* extra-marital sexual rompings, one-night stands, affairs, and other escapades, including "picking up" women at numerous public events, at least since becoming Arkansas' Governor. The most infamous was the affair President Bill Clinton admitted… with White House intern Monica Lewinsky.

Perhaps I should say that he only *semi*-admitted this, since he initially swore publicly that he "never had sexual relations with that woman." Oops!

"Bimbo Eruptions" aside, historically the word bimbo has been used with negative connotations and an air of disregard. Unfortunately, as many try to diffuse the stereotype, others try to hype it.

Back in 2008, a "Miss Bimbo" website sparked outrage, as the English and French Internet game encouraged girls as young as 9 years old to use dangerous diets and plastic surgery to get perfect bodies… all in an effort to create "the most beautiful, most wealthy, and most famous bimbo celebrity in the world."

Parent groups, medical experts, and psychologists all criticized the game as teaching young girls to honor and perpetuate a very negative and unhealthy stereotype. The game's creators argued that their virtual fashion game merely mirrored real life.

Sorry, game boys. Children cannot differentiate the sarcasm and humor. They take life at face value. While there has been a tendency to give feigned celebrity status to some people who have done nothing more than be socialites, "Miss Bimbo" game creators presented a very sad face that hardly reflects the real lives lived by most of us.

Tip: When misbehavers point the finger at victims, it does <u>not</u> transfer the blame to those victims.

4
I Can Relate

"If you would be loved, love and be lovable."
-- Benjamin Franklin (1706 – 1790)
USA Founding Father

Relationships are wonderful.

Relationships are painful.

Relationships are fulfilling.

Relationships are taxing.

Relationships are exciting.

Relationships are both complicated and comforting.

Relationships are annoyingly worthwhile.

Relationships are at the heart of all our dealings with people.

Our perceptions of the relevance of relationships vary dramatically depending on the state of our current primary relationship. Our own maturity also plays a powerful role in both our perceptions and in the ways in which we handle or mishandle our relationships.

We have all sorts of relationships throughout the various stages of our lives. With parents, siblings, and other relatives. With friends, neighbors, and classmates. With teammates, coaches, and teachers. With co-workers, customers, and supervisors. With our Lord.

Oh, yeah… and with girl/boyfriends, lovers, and spouses. And with offspring, stepchildren, and ex's. And more.

This book's primary focus remains on those relationships with "that special someone." The love relationships we want to have last forever… our beloveds. Whether we refer to them as boyfriends or girlfriends, lovers, partners, or spouses matters little. Just understand our words and stories as *your* personal situation dictates.

Sometimes we want our special someone to be very close. Sometimes we want to be alone. Sometimes we believe we'd be better off without any personal relationship with a lover ever again.

And yet, when we are most honest with ourselves, the vast majority of us want a strong, healthy, loving relationship.

As we look at big "oops" moments, disasters in the making, healthy struggles, and healing triumphs, you may well recognize yourself and a current or former lover in many of the scenarios.

That is good. We all need to know, especially when we flounder, that we are not alone. Others have been down these treacherous paths before us.

Human nature is not all positive. As a species, we have hardly evolved as far as we like to think we have evolved. Still, we are not on this journey alone.

Just like you, I have had good relationships and bad ones. I have been weak, and I have been strong. I have hurt, and I have been wronged. I have been happy, and I have suffered agony I wasn't sure I could survive.

Yet, just like you, I have survived. By sharing inner terrors, tips, and triumphs, we learn that caring and sharing helps us move from how to survive to how to thrive.

*"We are afraid to care too much,
for fear that the other person does not care at all."*
-- Eleanor Roosevelt (1884 – 1962)
American diplomat, activist,
and First Lady of the United States

Section 2
STEREOTYPING

5
<u>Keeping Up Appearances</u>

Real life is full of fake people.

In my earliest days of television journalism, I was asked to select a niche or two in which I had strong interest and knowledge. The entertainment and food fields felt equally appealing.

Of course, they'd likely meant some "hard news" theme, such as crime, politics, business, or even health.

However, I'd become a professional actress in the mid-1970's, and I am also a restaurant aficionado and gourmet cook with awards and numerous original, published recipes.

Cooking shows weren't yet "in vogue," but being a food / restaurant critic was AOK… except for one thing. I wasn't (yet) plump enough in management's eyes to have credibility as a food critic.

A stereotyped physical image (that I didn't seem to meet) negated my credentials and passion for food. Regardless, the state's first television Lifestyles / Arts & Entertainment reporter was born.

Later in my career, as the lead news anchor, I continued to break ground when new programming and time slots needed to be opened and developed.

This proved to be both fun and demanding. For example, for a live interview / news magazine program, I once learned I would be interviewing the author of a new book on the process of cold fusion the next day.

The book was HUGE and way over my head scientifically. I dove in. I had no choice.

After the interview, the author said he was amazed that I'd not only read the book overnight, but had been able to absorb the essence and talk with him using and explaining terms and concepts for the TV audience. He said all but trained scientists generally struggle with the extremely complex concept. Nice compliment coming from a man of his background… a man who was not at all disappointed at my non-scientific background or appearance.

Yayyy! Any of us who have felt the pangs of being the underdog relate heartily to a Bimbo not botching up high level interviews. Thankfully, I was blessed with awesome coworkers who cheered each other on in such endeavors.   We made a superb and strong team.

Success truly is the greatest proof of substance.

Never judge a book by its cover, right? Ah, human nature. We just can't help ourselves. And why not? Many people have landed… or failed to land… jobs based on appearance and other preconceived notions. This is not a news flash.

Over the years, I have known many people in media, in business, and in various other careers, who have taken steps to alter their appearance in attempts to alter public perceptions. The goal is to gain approval or likeability.

One female friend wanted to speak with a lower voice to boost her credibility.

Another donned glasses in an effort to look more learned.

A male friend shaved off his mustache after pollsters said that facial hair could give the appearance of hiding something.

One news director advocated wearing very conservative blazers, subtle colors, and only the tiniest of accessories, all to avoid the risk of offending any viewers. Likely, I offended him… daily.

In truth, we're always going to annoy somebody. It's the ol' "you can't please everyone all of the time" deal. It's too frustrating to *try* and please everyone anyway. We learn it is better to simply be the best we can be.

When we are true to ourselves, we are true to others, whether they like us or not.

Whatever field we may be in, keeping up appearances is something many of us do… to feel successful or on top of our game, to fit in or to mask personal weaknesses, to camouflage financial struggles or avoid looking like a "mess up" or a weak link at work.

To clearly see how avidly we work at keeping up appearances, we need only look at television or movies. The ripple effect of Hollywood into all layers of everyday society is mind-boggling.

I remember being stunned in 1983 in Los Angeles, California, while doing interviews for both news and a documentary. I learned that in the cities around Hollywood, more than 50% of young women had gotten breast augmentation by the age of 15. The effect already permeating local society would cruise coast-to-coast all too quickly.

The philosopher Aristotle is quoted as having said, "The aim of art is to represent not the outward appearance of things, but their inward significance."

Regardless, in the 21st Century, superficiality rules.

We dye away our gray hairs and have facials to try to keep our skin as youthful as possible. We also now see rapidly increasing numbers of women (and men) getting regular eyelash extension applications, Botox as early as the mid 20's, injections to boost cheekbones, not to mention breast implants and butt lifts.

Add to all that, procedures such as liposuction and a variety of new "freeze-the-fat" away techniques, hundreds of crazy diets, regular plastic surgery, and fashion emphasis with pressure to wear such things as 3-inch stiletto heels all day.

Regular media blasts push us to boost our beauty with new and improved products, fix our bodies with special, "secret" techniques, and wear the most hip clothes and hairstyles.

Perhaps the toughest toll is taken *inside* from the stress of trying to keep up whatever outward appearances we feel pressured to assume. We may feel over our heads in an academic class or overwhelmed in a work situation or simply uncomfortable in some social environment.

We've all learned the importance of appearing confident… like a duck gliding across the water, even if we are paddling like crazy underneath the water's surface. However, if we simply paddle till we drop, no one wins.

Tip: Don't let outward craziness dull your inner sparkle

6
Theories and Pseudo-Science

Moses led his people through the desert for 40 years.
It seems, even in Biblical times,
men avoided asking directions.

While stereotypes develop from both varying degrees of accuracy and constant repetition, many are so outdated that they become obnoxious and ridiculous because they are far off base for most people. On the other hand, though general, wide-sweeping statements are definitely exaggerated and do not apply to everyone, stereotypical statements are not always false.

Let's consider one stereotype. "Women are not good at math." Being a child of the 1950's, I grew up hearing lots of such statements. When compared to men, we were told that women score better on verbal sections of tests, and men score better in math sections. My math and verbal test scores often matched, or my math scores were much higher. Hah! Even my brain wanted to be defiant and go against tradition and science.

It could be true that people possess the ability to tap into *both* types of thinking or information processing with equal or near-equal success. Many times, we are simply not taught nor encouraged to *know* this, never mind encouraged to develop our abilities.

In junior high school in the 1960's, I was part of a 12-student test group given the high school Algebra I class. They'd hand-picked the students based on our math grades. The top students in the class were females.

No, I was neither <u>at</u> nor <u>near</u> the top. In fact, I was going through a particularly difficult time with my behavior. My acting out in class earned me my one and only "Academic Warning" that I would be getting a "C." My parents were not impressed.

My grandfather, a college math professor, said he'd tutor me. In our first afternoon, he found I easily did my algebra, as well as the advanced work he was giving to his students.

Math wasn't my problem. Attitude was a different matter.

By the time we graduated from high school, two of those same students from our early Algebra class became our Valedictorian and Salutatorian. Both were females. (No, I was neither one, although I had straightened out my wretched attitude.)

At the time, women were still often told that we supposedly did not *need* college, but if we wanted higher education, a study in liberal arts would be fine. We could choose nursing or teaching, of course.

I started college at Stetson University in DeLand, Florida, to my parents' chagrin, as a Speech and Theatre major. As a sophomore, I recognized that my presentation skills coupled with my math abilities made marketing and public relations a great career choice.

Switching to the business school would be no problem. However, I was not allowed to be a Marketing major. At the time, Stetson only permitted men in that program. They offered me their bachelor's degree program in administration / secretarial studies. Hellooooo! That was 1973. That was preposterous.

I transferred to Southern New Hampshire University (then called New Hampshire College). They didn't bat an eyelash when I asked to be a Marketing major. I didn't realize that I'd be the only female in my classes until I got into my classes.

Sure, I caught some sexist flak, but just from a couple of the professors. It was nothing I couldn't handle, and most of the faculty welcomed the program being co-ed.

No students gave me any grief. In fact, I became the first female to serve as president of the American Marketing Association's collegiate chapter.

Math and analysis courses were the easiest for me. This didn't help some classmates, since my scores of 100 meant that their Math or Quantitative Analysis grades couldn't be boosted on a sliding scale. I had one math professor ask to have my notes at the end of a semester, so he could use them as his teaching outline the following semester. That was flattering. That I was a woman mattered not one bit.

On the other side of that coin was a professor who was openly annoyed to have a female in her formerly all-male class. When semester grades came out she'd given me a "D." It didn't trouble me since I knew it was an honest mistake. I'd had an "A" average going into the final exam, and I knew I'd aced the final.

So, I went to her office. Her face was quizzical as she looked in her records. Then she calmly told me that she was unable to change the "D" based on my class participation. That stunned me, as I was one of the few students in her class that participated actively every day.

She replied that I'd had 3 absences, and my lack of participation on those days stood out. Say what? This was going nowhere. I lodged my formal complaint, and I moved on, avoiding classes taught by that particular teacher in the future.

Later, as a recruiter for the school, I helped women quickly become the majority in the Marketing major.

Today, marketing is very much a strong career field for women. We totally handle the quantitative requirements, while excelling in the multitude of communications arenas. Students today would likely be surprised to learn that it wasn't always a female-oriented, if not dominated, field.

Still, stereotypes get repeated so frequently, they can become their own clichés. Some clichés are funny. Some are ridiculous. Some are downright insulting. Often they are not even distantly related to the truth.

Here's another example. To this day I hear men moan and groan about how "women can't drive." (Oh, yes. My own loving husband is one of them.)

Regardless, studies and insurance company reports reveal that women are actually *better* drivers than men. Perhaps the stereotype evolved from past decades, when far fewer women drove, and the opposite may have been true.

Studies also find that men are more apt to engage in negative and aggressive driving behaviors, such as honking their horns at slower drivers, flashing their headlights with impatience, deliberately glaring at drivers they think are bad, speeding up to prevent someone else from passing, cutting in at the front of a merge situation (rather than waiting their turn in line), and chasing down a car when they think a driver cut them off in traffic.

We also hear that "women shouldn't be allowed to handle the checkbook." Despite warped past studies that tried to state that men were superior at balancing the books than women, it turns out that women are just as good at it as men.

In fact, when it comes to conscientiously paying bills, creditors state that their accounts with women tend to be paid on time regularly, while they find far more delinquent payments from men.

Further, they face challenges from men after late or failed payments. They report that these men offer all sorts of excuses and rationales, from the bill hadn't arrived on time to claiming that the accounts receivable department must have mishandled the payment. (Sounds like the dog ate my homework… again.)

Remember, however, these statements are <u>not</u> saying that <u>all</u> women are better drivers than all men, or that <u>all</u> women handle the checkbook and bill paying better than all men. These studies only indicate a majority… the typical findings. There are plenty of horrid drivers of both sexes, and there are plenty of men <u>and</u> women who remain clueless when it comes to handling money.

There are differences between men and women that do go beyond biological, such as the ways in which we communicate. In manufacturing products, designers tend to use colors, shapes, and lines they believe will appeal to the people who will be the primary purchasers or users of the products.

Studies show men tend toward darker colors and sharp, straight lines, while women like subtle shades, curves, and softer shapes. Then again, both sexes often fly directly in the face of such thinking.

However, here we are looking at the stereotypes that become exaggerations. Most hold a grain of truth… some carry lots of truth. As I have stated, some are humorous. Some are obnoxious. Let's just look at a few.

Try to see the humor, try to see the tragedy, and try to see the truth.

We probably all know people who fit some of the stereotypes perfectly. We also likely know people who are the opposite. (Some of these people may well be us.)

<u>**Male:**</u>
Boys wear blue and boots.
Boys play with trucks and action figures.
Boys like dinosaurs and jungle animals.
Boys play video games.
Boys should be tough and never cry.
Boys should learn to defend themselves.
Men know about cars, engines, and machines.
Men are good drivers.
Men can't raise children or are not responsible for their children.
Men are sports fanatics.
Men are mathematical and logical.
Men should be macho.
Men should be bread winners and providers.
Men are hunter/gatherers.

Men are bad communicators.
Men tune out their wife or girlfriend's voice.
Men should have fun, while women do the housework.
Men are impatient.
Men have bad memories.
Men should become doctors, not nurses.
Men don't care and are emotionally insensitive.
Men cheat on their spouses.
Men lie… often.
Men are fashion-challenged.
Men like camping and fishing.
Men should be in charge.
Men are dominant and tell their wives what to do.
Men are intimidated by strong women.
Men are not good with details.
Men are only interested in sex.
Men should not show emotion.
Men are lazy.
Men are couch potatoes.
Men like beer.
Men are messy.
Men are the best scientists and engineers.
Men do not like to cook or sew.
Men are sexist.
Men can't multi-task.

Female:
Girls wear pink and frills.
Girls are crybabies.
Girls tell tattletales.
Girls do not play video games.
Girls play with dolls and host tea parties.
Women all want to get married and have babies.
Women love babies.
Women are horrible drivers and can't parallel park.
Women don't need college.
Women should be ladylike.
Women should stay at home, cook, and do the housework.

Women should be happy housewives.
Women are illogical.
Women are overly emotional and care too much.
Women should be in the bedroom, not the board room.
Women who work should be secretaries, teachers, or librarians.
Women should be nurses, not doctors.
Women are shallow, ditzy, and fickle.
Women are self-centered and weak.
Women nag and are bitches.
Women are gossips.
Women get hysterical and are drama queens.
Women who are pretty are slutty.
Women should make less money than men.
The best mothers are stay-at-home moms.
Women are neat and tidy.
Women don't play sports and are bad athletes.
Women should not be politicians.
Women should be seen and not heard.
Women should be submissive and do as they are told.
Women lack technical ability.
Women should play the damsel in distress, but not the hero.
Women should look pretty.
Women love to shop.
Women love singing and dancing.
Women are flirts.
Women should never be in charge.
Women mistake sex for love.

In truth, it would be nice if we did not perceive most stereotypes as positive or negative. They are just reflective of tendencies and behaviors that may *be* or may have *been* typical.

We humans tend to be highly judgmental though. We can say that we don't care what someone's favorite hobby or color is, but little boys find themselves shunned or bullied by their fellow boys if they play with dolls or like the color pink.

Little girls who climb trees or play with trucks are labeled as "Tom boys," as if this is a negative connotation. Peer pressure pushes us to adhere to "perception-approved" choices and behaviors.

Before we can stop applying foolish stereotypes to people, we will need to stop teaching them to the newest generation of children.

Most people probably "get it" that stereotypes do not apply to everyone. Most people also understand that there is a bit of truth in stereotypes, which is how they became stereotypes in the first place.

It's challenging when popular television shows, both sitcoms and dramas, play up negative stereotypes. Often this is done in the name of comedy, and this has gone on since the advent of TV.

"I Love Lucy" featured Lucille Ball as the beautiful, but ditzy housewife. "Father Knows Best" taught men that there was something wrong unless they were the happy breadwinner, handling all of life's challenges with calm wisdom. Even old stand-by shows like "Leave It to Beaver" and "Dennis the Menace" taught kids that getting into mischief was fun and made you popular.

In programming of today, we now add floods of advertising, video games, and the Internet perpetuating stereotypes. Beer-bellied buffoons get the sexy chicks. Savvy career women can't find decent husbands. Men are presented as dumb jocks, incompetent husbands, insensitive jokesters, couch potato lumberjacks, self-centered metrosexuals, silent brooders, arrogant success types, cheaters, liars, slobs, and male pigs.

Women are portrayed as dumb blondes, prudes or sluts, happy or heinous housewives, sexy support staff, damsels in distress, overbearing bosses, sex kittens, pushy bitches, or mama bears filled with baby lust.

The lists go on and on.

I, for one, find that I can't even stomach previews for some prime-time television shows due to the ridiculousness, negativity, or offensiveness of the stereotyped characters. These are not the exception; they are often prime characters. Script writers have characters regularly saying negative things, supporting the thinking that they are funny by adding laugh tracks. What we may not realize is that we are spreading and supporting outdated, aggravating, and offensive stereotypes.

I am not suggesting that anyone stop watching programs that make them laugh. We simply need to recognize the development impact these images have on our young people.

Tired clichés can be sexist, ego-busting, and reality-warping.

It helps when we realize how stereotypes affect our expectations of each other. Whether we intend to or not, a human tendency is to put each other in specific "little boxes."

For most of us, this starts at birth. Well-intentioned parents dress girl babies in pink and lace, decorated with flowers, butterflies and little bows. They dress boy babies in blue and denim, decorated with sail boats, vehicles, and jungle beasts. Little girls are taught to be ladylike and not get dirty. Little boys are told to get tough and not be cry-babies.

In school, we typically succumb to peer pressure to "fit in" and be accepted or liked. Or we fly in the face of what appears to be "the norm" in an attempt to stand out or feel special or unique.

Pressure is particularly high while in school, where both boys and girls are struggling for individuality AND to fit in with their peers. It may start off with dressing or looking a certain way and evolve into being cool or not.

Far too frequently, failing to be accepted leads to bullying… sometimes extreme bullying.

We are all born loving, expression-filled humans, but we are taught how to "fit" our behaviors and responses into the "boxes" that society or our particular neighborhood peer group expects.

Boys learn such things as masking emotions and behaving as strong, masculine men. Girls are taught to soften physical strength and behave as delicate young ladies.

But everyone, pardon the generalization, has both traditionally "masculine" and "feminine" traits.

We need to develop awareness of the realities of men and women… and the associated stereotypes. For example:

Not all wives are chatter-boxes or nags.
Not all husbands are insensitive or slobs.
Not all men refuse to ask directions.
Not all women try to open doors with a smile.
Not all men turn into wimps at the slightest hint of sickness.
Not all women are spatially challenged.
Not all men joke to mask their insecurities.
Not all women obsess about dieting.
Not all men feel obligated to fight other men to feel manly or be adored by women.
Not all women manipulate men to get their way.
Not all men hate going to the mall with their wives or talking about emotionally mature facets of human nature.

Society is just learning to support a full spectrum of thinking, feeling, and behaving. It may take years, even generations, but we can all help by trying *not* to perpetuate negative stereotypes.

Tip: Try not to be a "stereotyper."

7

<u>Quips, Clichés and Other Obnoxiousness</u>

"If I made a joke about just dropping by,
would you write me off as cliché?"
— Cassandra Clare (1973 -)
American author in *"City of Ashes"*

A woman may hide her past from a man. A man hides her future.

The end of a relationship isn't the worst thing.
It's worse when it doesn't end after the end.

How can men and women understand each other
when they want different things?
A man needs a woman and a woman needs a man.

A woman never forgets a man that she was happy with…
A man never forgets the women he failed to have.

When a woman says that she'll be ready in 10 minutes, she is measuring time the same as a man, when he is says that the game will be over in 10 minutes.

Don't worry if you had a bad day –
just remember, that some people have
the name of their Ex's tattooed on their bodies.

When a woman falls in love, no one knows it, except herself. When a man falls in love, everybody knows it, except her.

He Said

When people ask me why I don't have any tattoos I reply:
Would you put a bumper sticker on a Ferrari?

Men are born between women's legs, and they spend the rest of their lives trying to get back there.

You need to carry women in your arms;
they will climb on your back by themselves.

Wife: "Darling, what are you thinking about right now?"
Husband: "If I wanted you to know, I'd say it, not think about it."

It's not a flaw to have a husband,
but an essential drawback to have a wife.

She is not my reward, but I am her punishment.

Husbands never have cash – they are married.

If a woman has fallen – an idiot will walk by, a gentleman will help her to get up, but a he-man will lie down with her.

Man's appearance is not the most important thing.
There are worse flaws.

If a woman is cold as a fish, a man must be as patient as a fisherman.

The Bimbo Has Brains

I never could bring a woman into my house.
At first, because of my parents. Later, because of my wife.

I only want a woman by my side from sundown to sunrise.

There is nothing more mean than cheating on a woman.
But nothing is more fun if you succeed.

You can't choose the right key to a woman's heart? Try choosing a key for some other place.

If it's getting cramped in the closet,
you should look for a new hiding place.

A confused man is someone who would die for his woman, rather than live with her.

If a wife is asking for something,
you could disappoint her so that she won't notice it.

If you want to be TOGETHER, you have TO-GET-HER.

If a man wants an angel in his life,
he first should create a paradise on earth for her.

If a man treats his girlfriend as a princess, it means he was raised by a queen.

If you are having a dispute with a woman and you hear her saying "WOW," you should run.

A real Don Juan must be able to dress both tastefully and very quickly.

It's uncomfortable when the neighbor's kids look like you.

You should sleep with a woman as though it's the last time.

Sex to a man is like hunger. If he can't get into an expensive French restaurant, he will go to a McDonald's.

Never go to bed with a woman that has more problems than you.

Everything is in the hands of a man. That's why you should wash them more frequently.

Have a woman that everyone else dreams about,
but don't dream about a woman that everyone else has had.

Men live better than women. First of all, they get married later and secondly, they die earlier.

A man never chooses a woman;
he gives her a chance to choose him.

Transitional age is when it's a hot day, but you can't decide what you want – ice cream or beer.

There are two types of guys: those who pee in the shower and those who don't admit it.

The wife of my friend is not a woman to me.
But if she's pretty, he's not my friend.

A bachelor lives like a human, but dies like a dog.

When looking at a woman an old man remembers.
A young one wishes.

Real men don't cry…tears for real men are unnecessary liquids in the body.

The difference between a fiancée and a wife is about 20 pounds.

The 10 dollars that neither your wife nor the tax collector knows about is worth far more than the 100 dollars that they both know about.

A wife in big doses is poison. In small doses she is medicine.

You should argue with your wife only when she's not around.

It's good when your wife is a master in the kitchen,
a lady in the living room and a whore in bed.
It's bad when she's a lady in the kitchen,
a whore in the living room and a master in bed.

If you want to marry a beautiful, a smart and a rich woman – marry three times.

Every wife should understand one thing.
Dinner will taste better if she cooks it less frequently.

A young housewife should learn that a small bottle of vodka will decorate the table. It will also hide any cooking mistakes.

If a wife is silent and not arguing – it means she's sleeping.

If your wife is holding a rolling-pin in her hands, it does not necessarily mean that she made pie.

Nothing irritates a woman more in a man's appearance
than the lack of money.

It's easy to make a woman happy, but it's not cheap.

If women didn't exist, all the money in the world wouldn't make sense.

Arguing with a woman is like a visit to the dentist. It's either very painful or very expensive.

A woman is helpless until her nail polish is dry.

Any skirt looks good on the back of the chair.

The Bimbo Has Brains

A man chases after a woman, just until she catches him.

She's a crabby woman when she doesn't like drunk men, and sober men don't like her.

A woman is like a parachute.
She can refuse to open at any time;
that's why you need to have a spare one.

You need to love a woman, not try to understand her.

Sex for a man is a goal and a tool for a woman.

A woman is a weak, helpless creature from whom you cannot save yourself.

A tattoo on a woman's ass: 'Best b4 Jan 1, 2020'.

Mosquitoes have more humanity than some women.
Mosquitos drink your blood silently.

A stupid woman holds her man by the throat.
A clever one holds him by the hand.
The wise one doesn't hold fast at all.

She Said

Only a widow can say exactly where her husband is.

Most men believe that women dream of having two men at the same time. What they don't understand is that in those fantasies one man is cleaning the house and the other one is cooking.

Dear men, if you stop seeing your wife as a lovely woman, it does not mean that all men are as blind.

If at first you don't succeed, try doing it in the way your wife asked. You may be amazed.

My ex sent me the following text message: "Can you delete my number? "

I responded: "Who is this?"

Female problems are nothing compared to male ones, from which the female ones were born.

Men always go to the left because women are always right.

What four-letter word does every man fear? More.

Most men are like frogs. They think the most important thing is to jump on faster.

Don't judge women by pounds, and you won't be judged by inches.

I have two questions. The first is, where have you been all my life?
The second is, would you please go back there?

If you want to marry a handsome, an intelligent, and a rich man –
marry three times.

Mostly men lie before elections and sex.
They also lie after fishing and cheating.

Men should be like coffee: strong, hot and not let you sleep all
night. However, most of them are like copy machines: suitable only
for reproduction.

What does a stork say after he brings the baby?
Nothing. He just rolls over and falls asleep.

Men hate two words: 'not' and 'enough'… unless you say them
together.

When a man claims that he has no bad habits, it means he is also impotent.

Men are like Bluetooth. When they're close, they're connected.
When they're away, they immediately look for new equipment.

It's better to be the first lover than the third wife.

I don't need Google. My husband knows everything.

A woman can fake an orgasm.
A man can fake an entire relationship.

If a man is cheating on you, it means he's indifferent to you.

God created a man.
Then, knowing that he could do better, he created a woman.

I am a virtuous woman. That's why I cost more!

Even a snow woman will melt if you keep cuddling with her.

Dear ladies, if you want to have more free time and have fun on the weekends, teach your men fishing!

A girl has to get in bed before 8 p.m. so she can come home by 11.

It is better to be in seventh heaven than in the seventh month.

Dear men, have you noticed that no woman ever started an argument with
a man when he was cleaning the dishes, vacuuming the carpet, or dusting?

Just because I'm smiling, it doesn't mean that I would not love to hit you in the face.

8
Heroes and Heroines

*"A hero is an ordinary individual who finds the strength
to persevere and endure
in spite of overwhelming obstacles."*
-- Christopher Reeve (1952 – 2004)
American actor

Heroes give us hope. Heroes reflect the very best of human nature.
Heroes go above and beyond in the attempt to accomplish what
needs to be done, despite personal risk. A hero may be a man or a
woman. They can be young or old. They could be military, first
responders, teachers, business people, parents, or neighbors. They
seek no reward. They inspire. They do what is right… and then
some.

I do not put superstar athletes or movie stars in the hero category.
While often idolized by fans for doing their jobs, neither their
careers nor their celebrity status qualify them for any sort of hero
status.

Work in most jobs does not automatically qualify as above-and-
beyond or life-saving. Then again, there are some celebrities who *do*
step above the rest by setting inordinately positive examples or
working to help improve society or boosting the next generation.

Sometimes heroism happens inadvertently or almost by accident.
Being in the right place at the right time, however, does not
guarantee we will *do* the right things.

Heroes do the right things. They make a difference. Sometimes
their sacrifice to make that difference costs them their lives.

Books are full of stories about heroic deeds done by people, and
even animals, in highly threatening situations. Sometimes
hundreds or thousands of people's lives were saved.

Heroes and Heroines

Heroic actions have occurred regularly throughout history. We often relate heroes and heroic actions to men. In truth, women have played strong roles as leaders and heroes, despite our Western European slant emphasizing male domination in leadership roles.

Women in celebrated and highly successful leadership roles have ranged from Queen Elizabeth I and Catherine the Great to Margaret Thatcher and Madeleine Albright.

Powerfully heroic social-action heroines include women like Pocahontas, who is credited with saving Captain John Smith, Mother Teresa, noted for her tireless work helping starving children, and Susan B. Anthony, an early leader in the movement to secure the right to vote for women.

Consider Joan of Arc, burned at the stake though she fought to save France in the Hundred Years War, and Rosa Parks, for sitting at the front of the bus, becoming a shining symbol of efforts to end racism.

Helen Keller is hailed for championing the rights of people with physical handicaps.

 We salute Amelia Earhart as the first woman to fly solo across the Atlantic Ocean in the early days of flight.

Coco Chanel was a hero in her own way, rising from a poor, starving waif of a girl to become a superstar designer and champion of women.

Real-life heroes and heroines have broken ground, made history, improved nations, advanced societies, saved lives, made vital medical break-through discoveries, and so much more.

I recognize that we aren't all cut out to be heroes, but I stand in awe and admiration of those who are. I believe it was American cowboy humorist, Will Rogers, who said, "We can't all be heroes, because someone needs to stand on the roadside to clap as the heroes march by."

Call me sappy, but I am one of those who gladly applauds and cheers, with tears running down my cheeks, when our military units pass in a parade. I just can't help it!

Back in the days of silent movies, women actually outnumbered men as the stars in action hero films. In the early 1900's, actresses like Mary Fuller, Grace Cunard, and Pearl White ("The Perils of Pauline") reigned in heroic roles that were bold and self-reliant.

Then Douglas Fairbanks swash-buckled his way onto movie screens in the 1920's and 30's. Our love affair with action heroes and heroines has never waned.

There's a long list of actors who've parlayed playing heroes into successful careers. Clever, witty types are fun, like Michael Weatherly. Everyone seems to have film favorites, like John Wayne, Arnold Schwarzenegger, Tom Cruise, Bruce Lee, Chuck Norris, Clint Eastwood, Bruce Willis, Danny Glover, Keanu Reeves, Matt Damon, Jason Statham, Steven Seagal, Harrison Ford, and Sylvester Stallone. I can't leave out my all-time favorite James Bond actor, Sean Connery. Many actors, like Johnny Depp, Dwayne Johnson, Brad Pitt, and Russell Crowe, manage to play both heroes and villains to equal accolades.

One can't help but notice that television and films in the last half century tend to feature male-dominated action hero roles. Sigourney Weaver stood alone for quite some time for her role as Ellen Ripley in "Alien." Plenty of badass babes have ruled the silver screen since. Consider the combat savvy of Carlie-Ann Moss as Trinity in "The Matrix" movies. Linda Hamilton's portrayal of Sarah Connor in "Terminator 2" also rocked.

Uma Thurman's character of The Bride in "Kill Bill" didn't speak a lot of lines, but she took motivated violence to a new level. The list goes on and on, from Milla Jovovich's Leeloo in "The Fifth Element" and Zoe Saldana's Neytiri in "Avatar" to Charlize Theron's portrayal of Furiosa in "Mad Max: Fury Road."

Angelina Jolie has ruled the list of badass babes with various roles, particularly her Lara Croft in "Tomb Raider." Another classic movie heroine is Katniss Everdeen played by Jennifer Lawrence in "The Hunger Games."

These actresses and more prove again and again that action heroines are fearless, resourceful, physically strong, independent, tactical, disciplined, self-reliant, and courageous. Their characters prove women need not be the damsel in distress. In fact, they save the men in trouble.

Television characters have also featured women in roles as action heroes. Emma Peel in "The Avengers" was an early classic, followed by the likes of Wonder Woman in "Wonder Woman," Jaime Sommers in "The Bionic Woman" and Xena in "Xena: Warrior Princess."

Consider Buffy Summers in "Buffy, the Vampire Slayer," Dana Scully in "The X-Files," Detective Olivia Benson in "Law and Order: SVU," Nikita in "Nikita," Detective Kate Beckett in "Castle," Agent Peggy Carter in "Agent Carter," and Ziva David in "NCIS."

While comic book and animated action heroes lack "realism," they represent fantasy heroes, saving people, cities, even the world and civilization from the destruction of evil forces everywhere.

2012's animated film "Brave" featured a sassy character named Merida. Her billowing red hair and fiery spirit won audiences' hearts with her determination, savvy, and heroic skills.

Comic books have featured a vast array of action heroes and heroines for decades, battling hate-filled Nazis, heinous aliens, and a host of other crazy fiends, all to save the world, yet again. Fans have their favorites, many of whom have crossed over into films, television, and video games.

Who can forget X-Men's Storm, Batgirl, Elektra, Black Canary, Catwoman, The Invisible Woman, the Avenger's Black Widow, Mina Harker (leader of the League of Extraordinary Gentlemen), and Natasha Irons.

The list of male comic super heroes runs even longer. It includes classics like Batman, Superman, Spider-Man, Green Lantern, Tarzan, Daredevil, Aquaman, Captain America, Ironman, Thor, Wolverine, the Incredible Hulk, Hellboy, and many more.

Teams of heroes also capture attention, from Guardians of the Galaxy and The Avengers to Teenage Mutant Ninja Turtles and the X-Men.

Many people enjoy action and super heroes, both male and female. People typically don't believe that they could literally possess superhero skills like the ability to have x-ray vision or climb buildings or fly, but we enjoy the fantasy characters because these stories usually have themes of good over evil and happy endings even after horrendous challenges.

For me, these are positive influences. Some argue that they present negative stereotypes that should not be presented to children.

Okay, the women get presented as anorexic, overly beautiful, and ultra-sexy. The men can be overly muscular, brooding, and violent. But they all tend to have very good hearts and morals, despite often coming from tough beginnings or having survived horribly difficult challenges. I fear critics focus on one stereotype that they find negative and miss many traits that we would applaud having young people emulate.

The problems come when we fight against stereotypes so strongly and fiercely that we end up trying to prevent people from being who *they* want to be and making choices *they* want to make. For example, what if a girl *wants* to wear pink and lacy frills and play with dolls and host tea parties for her stuffed animals?

Perhaps a little boy *wants* to wear blue and boots and play with dinosaurs, trucks, and action figures. They should be encouraged to do so every bit as much as the child who is encouraged to make nontraditional or non-stereotypical choices.

Consider this. In February, 2016, news reports revealed that a daycare in Norway refused to allow the children at its Trondheim facility to take part in the annual Fastelavn celebration. Traditionally, children mark the end of the carnival celebration season by dressing up in costumes. The Vikåsen Institute board decided not to celebrate because they didn't like the costumes that so many of the children were selecting. *They* decided... *for* the children... that girls dressing up as princesses and boys dressing up as superheroes was "too reflective of negative stereotypes."
(Source: *The Local; news@thelocal.no* Accessed 04/14/16)

Officials stated that they did not like children being encouraged to follow traditional gender lines and behaviors. Oh, I understand. Why should the girls want to be pretty or the boys try to be tough? Or why should kids want to dress up as their favorite princess or action or animated heroes?

Perhaps critics could gain some perspective by realizing that action super heroes are not all angry, overly aggressive, violence-obsessed beasts. Not all princesses are spoiled bimbos, materialistic fools, or incapable, dependent opportunists.

I remember first getting involved in theatre and trying out for various parts in plays. It didn't take me very long to recognize that the pretty girls got the pretty parts. Those of us who weren't seen as the "princess type," were out of luck, unless we could also play the juicy character roles.

But hey, I quickly learned that playing villains, witches, and other scraggly characters was much more fun. At the same time, those of us who didn't fit the princess mold got real ego boosts when some occasion entitled us to dress up in those pretty, frilly dresses and feel like a princess or a heroine. That should not be wrong.

I get quite "put off" when critics spout on and on about their disgust when a blonde is cast as a Hawaiian, or an actor with a Caucasian complexion wins the part of someone from the Far East. In seriousness, perhaps that actor was simply the director's favorite choice, and an actor's personal coloring should not restrict their casting success.

No one seems to complain if someone with a dark complexion is cast in some non-traditional setting, such as Cinderella, for example. Fully Black productions of "Cinderella" and other stories and films have been produced. "The Wiz" became Broadway's hit Black variation on "The Wizard of Oz." Thus, actors with light complexions should not be criticized for landing non-traditional roles either.

In acting, I remember being cast as Lucky in the play, "Waiting for Godot." Lucky is a man. Did this mean I was preventing a male actor from having the role? Or when I portrayed middle-aged or elderly women during my 20's, 30's, and 40's, did that mean I was taking a role away from a woman of the character's actual age?

We never looked at it that way. As a character actress, I *usually* portray characters very much unlike myself. We call it acting.

When will we straighten out all this insanity and slant demanding "Political Correctness," or what I continue to call "Political Quackiness?"

We need to stop being so hyper-focused on gender, race, age, and sexual stereotyping. Live and let live for crying out loud. From my perspective, we've gone so overboard with attempts to not insult someone or stereotype something about them that divisiveness is now the rule… far too often.

I love being married.
It's great to find that one special person
who will annoy you for the rest of your life.

Heroes and Heroines

When my husband and I dress up for masquerade or costume parties, we enjoy shaking things up a bit. On one Halloween, we cracked the other revelers up when we showed up as Mickey and Minnie Mouse. Our twist was that I portrayed Mickey, and I'd turned The Ronald into a 6'5" Minnie, complete with bloomers, petticoats, and golden pumps. He was an award-winning hoot-and-a-half.

At a pirate party, he went as an aging Captain Jack Sparrow and I as a battle-ready wench. Though, in our 60's and among the oldest attendees, we won the awards as Best Pirate and Best Wench.

It was not seen as a slight to the younger attendees. It was a credit to our costumes, make-up, and characterizations. We all celebrated and cheered for each other.

I think children should also be able to follow their own hearts and imaginations. If they fancy dressing up as particular characters, regardless of how popular, it should be encouraged and supported. When someone tries to dictate what is positive and negative for other people, they risk squelching creativity and free thinking. Most likely, this reigns as the exact opposite of what they mean to advocate.

It's high time we took active roles in what the next generation grows up believing to be "the norm" or even "okay." What if we stopped merely "accepting" what is handed to us by television, video games, and social media? What if we chose to not buy games or watch shows that present roles to which we object? What if we discussed stereotypes with each other and young people?

Tip: Try watching "questionable" material *with* your children, with the understanding that you will all sit down and talk about it afterwards. Calm perspectives and logic give them foundational understanding, without feeling shut off from programs or movies that may be popular with their peer group.

Section 3
FOR THE AGES

9
<u>Growing Older, Not Up</u>

> *"Age is a matter of mind over matter.*
> *If you don't mind, it doesn't matter."*
> -- Mark Twain (Samuel Clemens)(1835 – 1910)
> American author and humorist

The longer we live, one truth remains. We *will* grow older, but we need not grow *up*. Preparing to play the role of Peter Pan on stage was fun, and yet, as with most of us, the yearning to be Peter Pan-like *off* stage seems to increase with age.

As a child, we proudly announce our age, adding on the months since the last or until the next joyous birthday.

"I'm 7 years old and 4 months!"

"I'm 8-and-a-half."

"I'll be 16 in 2 months."

As an adult, we start to shy away from announcing or sometimes even acknowledging our age… at least not out loud. Then, if we think we still look pretty good for our age, we might be okay with people knowing we are middle-aged.

Once we become senior citizens, however, we start to get proud of our age again. It's as if being "of a certain age" gives us a special library card or hall pass to act out without getting in trouble.

"I'm just having a senior moment!"

"Okay, so, I'm a little eccentric."

"Hey, I've made it this far. What the heck?"

So, this chapter focuses first on some humor. Jokes come our way over the Internet, on television, in conversations, from magazines, and many other sources. Hopefully, you'll enjoy a few new ones here.

****

Two girlfriends sat talking.
"It's true," said one. "The doctor told me that to stay young
I need to eat better and drink less."
"So, what are you going to do?" Her friend inquired.
Without hesitation, she answered, "Find a new doctor."

****

A distraught senior citizen phoned her doctor's office.
"Is it true," she wanted to know, "that the medication you prescribed
has to be taken for the rest of my life?"

"'Yes, I'm afraid so,'" the doctor told her.

There was a moment of silence before the senior lady replied,
"I'm wondering. Just how serious is my condition,
because the prescription is marked
'NO REFILLS'."

****

An older gentleman was on the operating table awaiting surgery.
He insisted that his son, a renowned surgeon,
perform the operation.
As he was about to get the anesthesia, he asked to speak to his son.

"Yes, Dad, what is it?"

"Don't be nervous, son. Do your best, and just remember,
if it doesn't go well… if something happens to me,
your mother is going to come and live with you and your wife."

****

The Bimbo Has Brains

The older we get, the fewer things
seem worth waiting for in a line.

****

Some people try to turn back their odometers.
Not me! I want people to know *why* I look this way.
I've traveled a long way, and some of the roads weren't paved.

****

When you are dissatisfied and would like to go back to youth,
remember Algebra and Geometry.

****

One of the many things no one tells you about aging
is that it is such a nice change from being young.

****

Being young is beautiful, but being old is comfortable.

****

First you forget names. Then you forget faces.
Then you forget to pull up your zipper.
(It's worse when you forget to pull it down.)

****

Life is a race where everyone is trying to lead,
though they want to finish last.

****

Death takes away the best people.
It means that I will live a long time.

****

Don't hurry to your own funeral.
They won't start without you.

****

"What's a hipster?" asked my four-year-old cousin.
"Someone who will wear something just to look different," I said.
"They'll often buy clothes in thrift shops and wear thick glasses."
My cousin whispered, "Is Grandma a hipster?"

****

"So, what do you think is the best thing about turning 105?" asked
the reporter of the old woman.
She simply replied, "No peer pressure."

****

Two guys, one old and one young, collide while pushing their carts around Wal-Mart.

The old guy says to the young guy, "Sorry about that. I'm looking for my wife, and I guess I wasn't paying attention to where I was going."

The young guy says, "That's okay. It's a coincidence. I'm looking for my wife, too. I can't find her, and I'm getting a little desperate."

The old guy says, "Well, maybe I can help you find her. What does she look like?"

The young guy says, "Well, she is 27 years old, tall, with red hair and blue eyes. She is very buxom and wearing no bra. She has long legs and is wearing short shorts. What does *your* wife look like?"

To which the old guy says, "Doesn't matter. Let's look for yours."

The Bimbo Has Brains

My memory's not as sharp as it used to be.
Also… my memory's not as sharp as it used to be.

****

In the hardware store, a clerk asked,
"Can I help you find anything?"
"How about my misspent youth," joked my husband.
Without hesitation, the clerk smiled and shot back,
"We keep that in the back,
between world peace and the winning lottery tickets."

****

Seeing her friend Patte wearing a new locket,
Cathy asked if there was a memento of some sort inside.
"Yes," said Patte, "a lock of my husband's hair."
"But Jim's still alive," Cathy noted.
Patte replied, "I know, but his hair is gone."

****

Three old guys are out walking.
One says, "Windy, isn't it?"
The second one replies, "No, it's Thursday!"
The third one chimes in, "So am I. Let's go get a beer."

****

Life is too short to worry about what others say or think about you.
Have fun and give them something to talk about.

****

There's no respect in gangs today.
They just drive by and shoot people.
Remember the old days, like in "West Side Story"?
They used to sing and dance with each other first.

Just as she was celebrating her 80th birthday,
our friend received a jury-duty notice.
She called the clerk's office to remind them that
she was exempt because of her age.
"You need to come in and fill out the exemption forms,"
the clerk said.
"But I filled them out last year," she replied.
"You have to fill them out every year."
"Why? Do you think I'm getting younger?"

****

Know how to prevent sagging?
Simply eat until the wrinkles fill out.

****

Value time!
It's the substance of which life is made.

****

If the music is too loud, chances are that you're too old.

****

As the hostess at the casino buffet showed me to my table,
I asked her to keep an eye out for my husband,
who would be joining me momentarily.
I started to describe him,
"He has gray hair, wears glasses, has a potbelly…"
She stopped me right there.
"Honey," she said kindly.
"Today is Senior Day. They all look like that."

****

The Bimbo Has Brains

"My parents didn't want to move to Florida,
but they turned 60, and that's the law."
—Jerry Seinfeld (1954 -)
American Comedian

****

"Poor old fool," thought the well-dressed gentleman
as he watched an old man fishing in a puddle outside the pub.
So, he invited the old man inside for a drink.
As they sipped their whiskeys,
the gentleman thought he'd humor the old man and asked,
"So, how many have you caught today?"
The old man replied, "You're the eighth."

****

Make the rest of your life the best of your life!

****

All joking aside now, in many societies, the more we age, the more respect we gain. Growing up, I was taught to "respect my elders."

I saw the concept delightfully in action, while working as a television news journalist. We were covering President Ronald Reagan's Super Power Summit with Mikhail Gorbachev in Moscow in the U.S.S.R. After meeting some of the Bolshoi Ballet's Berlioz Ensemble dancers, my producer, videographer and I were invited to dinner in their home.

Life was not easy in the U.S.S.R, but these families had gone all out. They'd stood in various lines at stores, as was often required then, to purchase chicken, cheese, and more of the most wonderful foods they could. Such a lovely evening we had.

One baby sat at our long table. To our great surprise, they gleefully fed her expensive caviar. Our hosts explained.

Caviar was seen as so nutritious that they loved to feed it to babies to start building their brain power at the earliest age possible. It was also served to special guests, which they considered us to be. Most importantly, caviar was especially revered for their most elderly citizens in respect for their wisdom.

The concept was beautiful. Elderly citizens had worked extremely hard. The next generation truly sat at their feet, hungering for their wisdom and waiting for their stories to be told. We should be as respectful.

I'll close this chapter with a touching sentiment that was emailed to me a couple of years ago. It's rather sweet, and has a wonderful message with a nice dose of perspective on valuing what is truly important.

****

At an airport I overheard a father and daughter in their last moments together. They had announced her plane's departure. Standing near the door, he said to his daughter, "I love you, and I wish you enough."

She said, "Daddy, our life together has been more than enough. Your love is all I ever needed. I wish you enough, too, Daddy." They kissed good-bye, and she left.

He walked over toward the window where I was seated. Standing there I could see he wanted and needed to cry. I tried not to intrude on his privacy, but he welcomed me in by asking, "Did you ever say good-bye to someone knowing it would be forever?"

"Yes, I have," I replied. Saying that brought back memories I had of expressing my love and appreciation for all my Dad had done for me. Recognizing that his days were limited, I took the time to tell him face to face how much he meant to me.

So, I knew what this man was experiencing. "Forgive me for asking, but why is this a forever good-bye?" I asked.

"I am old, and she lives much too far away. I have challenges ahead, and the reality is that her next trip back will be for my funeral," he said.

"When you were saying good-bye I heard you say, 'I wish you enough.' May I ask what that means?" He began to smile.

"That's a wish that has been handed down from other generations. My parents used to say it to everyone." He paused for a moment, looking up as if trying to remember it in detail. He smiled even more.

"When we said 'I wish you enough,' we were wanting the other person to have a life filled with enough good things to sustain them," he continued. Then, turning toward me, he shared the following as if he were reciting it from memory.

"I wish you enough sun to keep your attitude bright. I wish you enough rain to appreciate the sun more. I wish you enough happiness to keep your spirit alive. I wish you enough pain so that the smallest joys in life appear much bigger. I wish you enough gain to satisfy your wanting. I wish you enough loss to appreciate all that you possess. I wish you enough 'Hello's' to get you through the final 'Good-bye'."

He then began to sob and walked away.

10
Watch This!

*Think how much you could do
if you didn't care what other people think.*

Admit it or not, we have been seeking respect, awareness, and admiration since childhood. Whether you are near the merry-go-round at the carnival or on the deck of a hotel swimming pool, the air is filled with children's voices repeatedly calling out to parents to "Watch this! Watch this!" Or "Look at me!" They may be jumping into the pool for the 40th time. The repetition matters little. Children continually seek parents' attention and praise. This applies equally to boys and girls.

*Girls want attention.
Women want respect.*

This is not to imply that everyone *gets* the attention they need, never mind admiration, respect or appreciation. However, everyone *needs* and seeks it.

By high school, some kids have learned that they can earn some attention, admiration, and respect by excelling academically, athletically, or creatively. Others continue to seek attention by being the loudest or the funniest, by acting out badly, by other behaviors such as how they dress or wear their hair, or even by things they purchase, from special concert tickets to getting (and revving) that big engine in their car.

There are few, if any, guidelines on how to positively evolve our respect-, awareness-, or admiration-seeking models into patterns that work effectively in relationships.

One thing none of us wants, however, is to find that someone *else* is telling the person you love that they are capable, attractive, exceptional, amazing, appreciated, sexy, hard-working, or that they simply can't believe that YOU don't see these things in your mate.

Be sure that you frequently observe the person you love so that you can and *do* share with them how proud you are of their efforts, how much you appreciate their positive attitude, how great it makes you feel to be out in public with them because they always try to look their best for you, and so forth.

We never want to become so close to someone that we forget or become unable to see their precious value.

On the other hand, there are always those people who will take advantage of you and your kindness and respect. You keep totally on top of your game. You try hard to stay in shape and look your best for them. You work hard. You help provide a comfortable and welcoming home. You let them know they are loved and appreciated. They, unfortunately, take *this* for granted… and a lot *more*. They have made a conscious or unconscious decision to take what they can get from life without any genuine intention of giving back in kind.

There are names for people like this… players, cheaters, takers, frauds, and such. I remember the old 1966 hit song, "The Cheater," sung by Walter Scott, the front man with Bob Kuban and the In-Men. I believe it was written in 1965 by their bass player, John Michael Krenski.

The song may have made the group a one-hit-wonder, but the sentiments to beware of the inevitable hurt bestowed by cheaters, players, and takers is timeless.

Whether we like it or not, some people get their kicks by playing on the vulnerabilities of others. They take. Then they move on… to their next victim.

A mistake is an accident.
Cheating and lying are not mistakes.
They are intentional choices.
Don't hide behind the word "mistake"
when you get caught!

Try to avoid people who use people. If you are in an unhealthy relationship, you can only control your *own* attitude, actions, and responses.

However, doing the right things and setting the right example might help your partner get "healthier" themselves. Still, if they *don't* make those choices, it's not *your* fault. If you love them, treat them as you would like to be treated. Meet their needs to the best of your ability.

If we want our most important relationship to thrive, we each must take personal responsibility, regardless of our partner's choices. Show respect and speak with appreciation. Give them "the look" that says, "You're the greatest."

Use words that share how lucky you truly do feel to be with them. Recognize the value they bring to the relationship and tell them that you couldn't do it without them. Use the three words, "I love you" daily.

Tip: Share four other important words: "You make me proud."

11
<u>Freaking Out</u>

A powerful control freak may get you opportunities you might not otherwise likely get. However, because of a control freak, you might not be able to take advantage of opportunities you get.

We can all be controlling now and then, but for some of us, it's a way of life we either live ourselves or have someone laud over us. Control Freaks are specialists at throwing their weight around lovers, spouses, co-workers, and even their children. Control Freaks typically do not recognize that they are seen by others as Control Freaks.

In fact, Control Freaks often label *other* people as Control Freaks. This is usually to deflect their own insecurity and frustration at not being able to more readily control someone.

A Control Freak often puts a spouse down until getting their way. They frequently get angry if their partner disagrees with them.

A Control Freak commonly doesn't like a spouse to see his or her own family. A Control Freak readily accuses his lover of being a flirt or having an affair, when it's the Control Freak who needs to look in the mirror.

It takes a great deal of compassion to deal with a Control Freak. They very easily get angry and defensive. When confronted by their hostilities, don't go toe-to-toe. Stay calm. Speak slowly and softly. Try to keep your sensibilities and humor.

I harken back to Jeff Foxworthy, a comedian known for his insights into why "You Might Be a Redneck." One big difference is that Control Freak comedy is pathos.

It helps when we can look at tough scenarios in life with at least a slice of humor, especially if we are on the receiving end of "Control Freakdom." If we don't see ourselves in several of the following, we might not be human. With emphasis on loving relationships, here now is a look at why "You Might Be a Control Freak."

For example, if you believe that to get something done right, you usually must do it yourself… you might be a Control Freak.

If you know people actually *need* you to keep an eye on them… you might be a Control Freak.

If you worry that your lover will hurt you or leave you…

If you believe you are helping others when you make decisions for them…

If you get annoyed when your partner makes a decision for herself (or himself) without seeking your input first…

If you regularly drive aggressively…

If you've been told not to micromanage someone or some situation, even though you believe you weren't micromanaging…

If you wish your husband or wife would just *please* do something right for a change…

If you blame others for your problems…

If you are finally ready to go somewhere and don't understand why everyone else isn't already sitting and waiting in the car…

If you blame or yell at your spouse first when something goes wrong or seems to be missing…

…you might be a Control Freak.

If you can't stand talking to telephone customer service representatives and often end up yelling at them…

If you think that while on a flight, shutting off your cell phone audio, never mind your cell phone, is a rule for *others* to follow…

If your partner's calendar, appointments, or commitments lack priority to you, or they can and should be cancelled if you come up with something more important for them to do…

If you struggle with commitments…

If you criticize, belittle, or minimize something your partner has achieved without you…

If you are good at manipulating others to get your way…

If you sulk or act annoyed or unenthusiastic when you "let" your partner have their way on something…

If you know what's best for your lover…

If you doubt your spouse's sincerity or decision-making capacity…

If you struggle to compromise because you know the other side is weak, imperfect, or not adequate…

If you expect other people to answer *your* questions, but ignore your own *spouse's* questions…

If you try to make your lover (or even your adult children) feel dependent on you…

If you have internal challenges but tell your spouse that he or she needs to seek professional counseling…

…you might be a Control Freak.

If you need to see it to believe it...

If you can't be a passenger and let others drive the car...

If you are known as someone who frequently complains...

If you blame the failure of a product or tool you are using when you are struggling to fix or do something...

If you need to win every argument...

If you are filled with anger, anxiety and insecurity...

If you have a lot of internal fear...

If you can't stand how so many bad drivers always seem to end up right in front of *you* on the road...

If you need to know your spouse's "sign on" and passwords, but don't openly share yours...

If, when you're away, you call and check in to be sure your spouse got home from work in a timely manner, while *you* go out at night...

If you are really tough to please...

If you behave aggressively and easily lean toward confrontation...

If you apply double standards in your relationship (she shouldn't go to bars without you, but you go without her... or he shouldn't shop without you, but you shop without him, etc.)...

If you are someone who frequently sends meals back in a restaurant...

...you might be a Control Freak.

If you get grumpy or find some excuse to be ticked off after your spouse has had fun or done something without you…

If you don't like it when your spouse sees friends without you…

If you've gradually weaned your partner away from their friends, family, hobbies or favorite activities…

If you regularly cross the line between making suggestions and delivering controlling mandates…

If you give orders but don't readily share or delegate tasks…

If you get annoyed when your spouse keeps any secret or doesn't share information with you…

If you feel better when you weaken your lover…

If you are intolerant of other's lifestyles, choices, or viewpoints…

If you have accosted your lover with name calling or swearing…

If you've accused or picked on your spouse in public or in front of friends…

If your spouse has ever said that they feel as if they are walking on eggshells around you…

If you've ever used force or intimidation to make your point or get your way…

If you've ever thrown something at your lover…

If you've come up with rules your spouse should follow, even when the negative behaviors addressed actually apply to you…

…you might be a Control Freak.

If you generate a lot of stress in your spouse or others around you...

If your spouse says he or she prefers to talk about challenges *after* you've calmed down or stopped ranting or sobered up...

If you are unpredictable in private... run hot and cold, can be outgoing or withdrawn, or change from happy to angry in a flash...

If you fault others for your anger or outbursts...

If you lose your cool with your spouse, but control it around people you are trying to woo or influence...

If you are charming in public, but brooding or ambivalent behind closed doors...

If you feel bothered, troubled, or threatened by positive activities (reading, writing, working out, cooking, gardening, painting, playing music, etc.) your partner does to feel happy and fulfilled...

If you try to control others to prevent them from controlling you...

If you don't trust the judgment of even those you trust...

If you struggle to let someone else be in a position of control...

If you legitimately can't cast blame on your spouse for something, but you still manage to point the finger elsewhere...

If you believe that your spouse never listens to you, and if they <u>do</u> listen, they just do as they please anyway...

If you seek perfection in your spouse...

If you point out flaws in everything your spouse does...

...you might be a Control Freak.

If you believe you'd be happier if your spouse would even do just *one* thing you've asked…

If you make your partner feel as if he or she is a big disappointment to you…

If your spouse feels the need to ask your permission to do things (get a haircut, use the car, go to the grocery store, etc.)…

If you view your lover's belongings as clutter, but don't even see your own untidiness…

If you don't think that *you* have a problem, because someone *else* causes the problems…

If you need to set the "To Do" list priorities for your partner…

If you are secretly annoyed by or jealous of someone who does something better than you…

If you play mind games or sometimes make your spouse feel off balance or insecure…

If your spouse has ever expressed that you've made them feel helpless or isolated…

If you regulate your lover to avoid the pain or fear of being alone…

If you've ever used the "silent treatment" to make sure your spouse gets your point…

If you've been told that you drain happiness from or bring stress into situations…

If you get angry or annoyed if your partner tries to gently or lovingly point out something negative…

…you might be a Control Freak.

If you get defensive when anyone shares any criticism of you...

If your spouse made an error, and you never let them forget it...

If you are known as someone who is not good at apologizing...

If you don't need to hear the other side of the story...

If you absolutely hated this particular chapter...

And...

If you thought you were wrong once, but it turned out that you were mistaken...

...you might be a Control Freak.

In truth, it's natural to try to influence others to our way of thinking or behaving. We should all seek input, opinions, and suggestions. However, we should also only *offer* input, opinions, and suggestions with full respect for others to make their own decisions, even if they differ with the choices we wish they'd make.

We need to control ourselves and not try to control others. Trying to control others is not only rude and disrespectful, it's like trying to put toothpaste back in the tube or trying to push a rope. No matter how hard we try to teach a pig to sing, we'll only frustrate ourselves and annoy the pig.

Control Freaks have a great deal of trouble getting comfortable with the unknown. If you live with a Control Freak, you need a lot of savvy to not leap to their level when they try to confront, criticize or control you. However, just as *they* should *not* try to control their loved ones, *we* cannot force them to accept responsibility for their own happiness and other feelings.

Tip: Relax. None of us will get out of this Life alive.

12
<u>Laugh to Remain Ageless</u>

Life is short. Smile, while you still have teeth.

I admit it. My face has lines. I like to quip that I've earned each and every one of them. Life's experiences will do that to us.

As a high school girl first learning to apply stage make-up, our director, Marcelle Houle, taught us how to apply character lines. We'd scrunch our faces, furrow our brows, squint our eyes, or smile really broadly… then relax and quickly apply the dark grease pencil in the tiny, barely visible line that remained, but vanished in just seconds. Hello! I don't need to do any face scrunching any longer. The lines aren't so tiny, and they most assuredly do not disappear. My face has character. That is good, because I *am* a character. My face should match, and now it does.

Later, in college, I recall getting to know a lovely older woman. She wore her crystal white hair in a fancy up-do. She always dressed in very contemporary fashions. In fact, though it seemed out of character for her, she dressed like we in our late teens and early 20's dressed… right down to her knee-high, white, patent leather "go-go" boots. (Those became a fashion fad after Nancy Sinatra's hit song, "These Boots Are Made for Walking.")

However, it taught me what I did *not* want to emulate as I aged.

The older you get, the better you get,
unless you are a banana.

Few of us like the changes our bodies go through when we get older. Our bodies and faces can become unrecognizable, even to ourselves. It's one thing to say, "I refuse to grow up," but we can't help but grow older. Okay, okay, but I figured I could at least try to age gracefully. Growing older is destiny. Growing older gracefully is a choice… a choice I wanted to make.

I can remember a couple of friends having some plastic surgery when we were in our 20's. One suggested that I do it, too, since she knew a "nose job" would improve my face. I do have quite a honker, but I got used to it as I grew up. I figured that I would at least hold out till I was 50. Then, when I turned 50, I backed my timeline off to 60. Once into my 60's, I decided I would just forget about it. I've now seen far too many super-stretched, taut expressions and "mannequin faces" on women... and men... trying to cling to their youth.

I rather like my character... both inside and out. I think it was Ralph Waldo Emerson who said, *"Character is who we are when no one is looking."* I always liked that.

Laughter helped me not take myself so seriously, which helped my true character develop. Laughter also helps us move through the aging process, as well as other challenging phases of life.

There are plenty of jokes and one-liners to help, too. Here are some "lines" on aging. You know you are "old" when...
- The clothes you put away until they come back in style have come back in style.
- You wish you could iron your birthday suit.
- You can still chase the "good-lookers" but only downhill.
- The fortune teller reads your face instead of your palm.
- Your favorite TV station is The Weather Channel.
- You finally know your way around, but you don't want to go anywhere.
- The candles on your cake set off the sprinkler system.
- You still miss your high school car, but you can't remember your classmates.
- The old spark takes a little more blowing to get going.
- Your favorite classic rock song is now elevator music.
- Your childhood toys sell for a fortune on eBay.
- You count on getting lots of mail... from AARP.
- You're the life of the party, even if it lasts until 8pm.
- You know you wouldn't want to *be* a teenager again, but you wouldn't mind looking like one.

- You just can't stand people who are intolerant.
- You've started boring complete strangers with your medical problems.
- It's not the cop, but the doctor who's telling you to slow down.
- For breakfast you eat cereal instead of last night's chicken wings and leftover pizza.
- Your narrow waist and broad mind have traded places.
- It takes a couple of tries to get over a speed bump.
- It takes longer to rest than it did to get tired.
- You got your head together, but your body is falling apart.
- There's nothing left to learn the hard way.
- You're not cranky. You just don't like traffic, waiting in lines, crowds, loud music, unruly kids, barking dogs, politicians, and a few other things you can't remember.
- Your Sweetie says, "Let's go upstairs and make love!" And you answer, "Pick one. I can't do both!"

Yesterday, I fell down from a 30-foot ladder.
Thank God I was only on the third step.

I remember all the years when I'd work at least 60 hours a week. I always loved my work, but it sure could get in the way of living. If someone doesn't like their job, then the days and hours matter little. We are merely working to support our life… pay the rent and such. For others of us, working hard fulfills us. So, life is beautiful… from Monday to Friday, or whatever days we work.

In truth, we all need to keep a little perspective at every age in life. At any moment you find yourself feeling down, say a prayer. Call a friend who is a positive person. Pick up a book. Find something that can make you smile, if not laugh. It need not be something momentous.

Tip: Sometimes the slightest ray of sunshine warms the room.

Section 4
ATTITUDE

13
Save Face

*"Keep your face always toward the sunshine,
and the shadows will fall behind you."*
-- Walt Whitman (1819 – 1892)
American poet

This is more than a call to "save face." I should say save the faces….
And the sarcasm.

It's a squirrely part of human nature, I guess, that makes many of us
behave nicer with people we don't even know than we do with
people we love. This can happen to any of us.

Sir Ronald and I finished working on our afternoon projects one
Saturday, and he was tuning his sound system. I put away the
groceries and asked him if he wanted the chicken that I had bought
or if he preferred something else for dinner. Hubby said he wanted
the chicken.

It was 6 o'clock, so I prepared dinner and set the table. I skipped
the small talk, though he was standing only about 20 feet away
from me. He seemed focused on his electronic adjustments.

Just before serving time, as usual, I asked him if he wanted a bottle
of water with dinner. He said he'd prefer a glass of wine and added
that there was some in the refrigerator. I poured his wine and put it
at his place setting. I then asked if he was ready to eat.

Eek! I guess not. He made his famous "hate" face, rolled his eyes,
and steamed, "No!" He then added, "But I guess if you're hungry
we have to eat."

I said, "Woah! Save the faces, the eye-rolling, and the sarcasm. A
simple 'not yet' would be fine. No big deal; just tell me."

I shut off the oven. No problem, right?

Now, wouldn't it have been more pleasant for both of us, if he'd communicated differently at the start? For example, when he told me that he wanted the chicken, he could have added something like, "How 'bout we plan to dine around 7 or 7:30?"

I mean, I was preparing everything right in front of him. Unless he said something, how else would I know he did not want to eat yet? We had eaten a very light brunch at noon. I thought that prepping for 6:30 dining would be fine.

Often there are "indicator" or "warning" signs that someone has difficulty communicating with loved ones or responding appropriately. You may see that they jump to conclusions and don't back off, even when evidence clearly shows a different result. There may be snap judgments. They may simply speak very ill of people who they do not perceive as acting as *they* think that person *should*… without any consideration of circumstances.

* * * * * * * * * * *

Mary had been on a snow skiing date with her new fiancé, Marvin. They had both been married previously, and Marvin's teenaged children were with them. Driving away from the ski resort they headed to a local restaurant for dinner. As they approached a stop sign, Mary glanced to the right to look out the passenger's side window at the oncoming traffic.

"Wait, would you…" Marvin started with a snarl in his voice and on his face, as he reached his arm out and across her body. As Mary looked back, her eyes widened upon seeing his contorted face, which immediately softened into a smile.

He then simply and calmly said, "I just need you to sit back so I can see."

"Oh, I'm sorry," said Mary.

Immediately from the back seat came wails of disbelief from the kids. "Oh, no! I don't believe he just smiled."

Mary quietly commented, "You were going to yell at me?"

"Oh, no," Marvin replied.

"Oh, yes!" came the choral reply from the backseat. "I can't believe he backed off."

"He always yells."

"He sure would have yelled if it was one of us."

"Well," Mary started calmly. "Maybe he's handling things better these days, because yelling would have been a rather over-the-top response in this situation."

Years later, Mary spoke of the situation and recognized it as a warning that her husband had some "proper response issues." After they were married, sure enough, he started yelling at her with increasing frequency.

She knew they needed help when it grew to be out of control, complete with swings from "the silent treatment" to name calling, and from tuning out her voice completely to threatening her physically. As she put it, "This was all above my pay grade."

Whether someone responds to challenges with what I call "angry speak" or gives you "the silent treatment," they are refusing to participate in constructive communication.

We can call the behavior "childish." It is. Its origin likely stems from what was tolerated, what was observed, and what worked for them when they were young. If we recognize these things in ourselves, we need to work on them.

Some people think that it's okay to be downright nasty to people they love. It is *not* okay. Nasty is never called for, and it's certainly not sweet, useful, nor positive.

We should all be aware of phrases and statements that indicate highly disrespectful escalations in responses. For example, "If you do that again, I'll hit you."

That may sound overtly outlandish, but it happens more often than you might think. One woman noted a time when she and her husband were at a crowded bar. She was seated, and her husband was standing beside her, behind his empty bar stool.

A lady they didn't know was standing nearby.

The wife turned to her husband, quietly asking if he would like to offer the lady his stool, since he wasn't using it. He looked over and saw her. He then turned to the woman and invited her to sit down. She thanked him and sat.

Then he did something unexpected. He turned to his wife, leaned his face close to hers and hissed, "Do that again, and I'll hit you."

Seriously. From the start, he could have simply said, "Nah, I might want to sit down." His ultimatum was both out of the blue and outlandish.

Quite frankly, delivering *any* ultimatums is unacceptable. Period.

The same goes for increasing efforts to try to transfer negative behaviors to a spouse.

The wife at the bar told her out-of-line husband that his comment was totally inappropriate.

He retorted, "*You* were totally inappropriate. You'll never learn. You've *always* done this for years! I can't take it anymore."

In truth, if it isn't to save your life when it's in imminent danger, someone yelling at you is just plain wrong.

The same is true for ranting or bitching.

The same goes double for anything even close to manhandling.

There is never a worthy excuse… just an impatient, undisciplined abuser. If rantings escalate beyond a level that is tolerable to you or take the form of threats to you or your safety, get safe and get help.

Tip: A smile is the best thing we can wear. Without it, little else matters.

14
<u>Great Expectations</u>

Life is lived by optimists.
Pessimists are just viewers.

Making it real, starts with our attitude.

Marlene groaned, "Good grief! It's a mixed blessing, but I kid you not… Roger literally wants sex every day, even after 20 years of marriage! I'm a good sport, but sometimes one or the other of us just isn't up for it, no pun intended. This morning he even complained that he hadn't gotten 'his blow job' in two days. Like it's an expectation or something. What's a woman to do?"

I pondered her words and offered one of my more typical, albeit calloused, remarks. "Remind him," I suggested, "that you GIVE him a blow job. It's not *his* until you give it to him."

Sarcastic? Sure. But also, if a man or a woman starts "expecting" sex, then it is no longer special, and a lover *will* likely start to feel used.

Both partners in a relationship have needs, though they aren't always identical. With good communication and mutual respect however, everyone can be happy, and no one needs to feel compromised.

We also meet each other's needs through our attitude. Positive enthusiasm is good. Whining annoyance? Not so much.

An optimist believes that we live in the best world.
A pessimist is afraid that might be true.

If I make the bed each day, grumbling with reluctance, *that* reflects a bad attitude. My mother always gave me a clever choice. "You can make your bed with a smile, or you can make your bed with a frown, but you are going to make your bed."

Her rules ruled. My choice was how to respond.

Trust me when I tell you that I was quite a miserable handful as a child, but through adolescence I learned that Life is not only easier, but far more pleasant, when I make positive choices.

We are faced with opportunities to make positive choices every day. Take for example, commuting to and from work. On the road, the creepy driver who cuts you off might deserve your scorn.

Skip the urge to *respond* to a road rage invitation.

I find that my days are far more smooth and pleasant when I don't give someone the leverage to annoy or stress me. Just smile, giggle to yourself, or wave "hi" with a wag of your pinky finger, if you must. But then the incident is over, and no stress or annoyance remains, at least not in my car.

The self-centered driver has the negative attitude. Don't let someone else's poor behavior choices become contagious.

I am an absolute master
of doing the right things absolutely wrong.

Here's an even better example, as it deals with our personal relationships. My husband is an avid boater. He's known since we first started dating that I am a landlubber. Boating was not in my background, and I am not a fan.

We were living in New Hampshire, where the boating season on the state's largest lake, Lake Winnipesaukee, is rather short... May through October, at best.

So, with sweet summer days limited, going out on the boat every possible day is Hubby's idea of fun and relaxation. For me, boating every weekend swings between boredom and stress.

However, I believe deeply in supporting each other's passions. So, I have lots of choices.

That said, I could press my will on him and push to only boat for a certain number of days per week or month, giving us time to also enjoy other summer activities from the mountains to the ocean shore. I could let him boat without me, but that would be a drag because we enjoy being with each other and doing things together. I could boat with him, but let him do all the work involved, since it's "his thing." I could go along for the boating, but be grumpy and crabby and generally no fun. I could boat with him and "guilt" him, constantly reminding him that "I only do this for you." I could remind him how much money it costs us. I could go along but totally lack enthusiasm.

Why spoil his good time? Why be a cranky partner? Why belittle a passion of his? Why manipulate? Why set us up for relationship failure by opening the door for him to fill the boating gap with someone else?

Instead, he knows that I am not a boater, do not share his personal interest, and am actually scared of the water. He also knows that I am an enthusiastic joiner. I will make lemonade out of lemons and serve it with a smile… daily.

Some have asked how I do it. I make it a point to find the aspects that appeal to me, and I focus on those. I love being with Ron. I love the friends we have made while boating or dockside. I love when we stretch out on lounge chairs and bask in the warm sunshine.

I love entertaining both on the boat and dockside. I love preparing goodies to eat and share. I greatly enjoy prepping everything from breakfast to dinner dockside.

In fact, I love that so much that I've even released a "Dockside Dining" cookbook series. It's full of K.I.S.S.™ (Keep It Super Simple) recipes that work great on shore, on board, tailgating, and in the backyard.

Anyway, if I'm sitting dockside on a lounge chair, enjoying the morning sun, and he says to me, "What would you like to do today?"

"Um," I think to myself, "I'm doing it."

Actually, I've learned that's not really his question. He knows what I'd like to do comes from a long list of landlubber activities. I know he's really asking where I'd like to take the boat on that day.

When we make the decisions to *be* and *stay* in love, we should also make a decision and commitment to be supportive.

Deciding to be his gleeful Galley Girl easily became my "happy place" as First Mate for my Captain Ron. Joining, supporting, and contributing is far happier and healthier for both of us than me squabbling, blocking, or dragging my feet.

While I don't have any hobbies that wrap up that much of his time, he also gets opportunities to show support for my activities.

As an actress, it was tough for him to grasp even a 10-day rehearsal schedule, and the run of performances annoyed him, as he wanted to be doing other things.

It's a good thing he met me years after the long weeks of rehearsals in community theatre or professional musical touring companies. On the other hand, he always said that he absolutely loved seeing me on stage. So, we figured it out, and it worked, as long as I didn't do long runs or do it often.

I also love volunteering and being community-involved. While that's not "his thing," he has learned that it's fun and highly rewarding to get involved, as long as it's only occasionally.

In respect for the relationship, I dramatically reduced my civic commitments. Kept unchecked, I'd love nothing more than being a full-time volunteer "when I grow up."

I guess the key here is "balance." If he complained, blocked, and, thus, made my endeavors and commitments challenging to accomplish, this would be disrespectful of both me and activities I value, right? Right.

> Marge: *"Homer, is this how you pictured married life?"*
> Homer: *"Yeah, pretty much, except we drove around*
> *in a van solving mysteries."*
> -- Quote from "The Simpsons" animated television show

Now, when it comes to our expectations regarding intimacy, I believe in recognizing that both partners in a relationship have expectations and needs. As part of a loving, respect-filled team, these should be communicated supportively.

Remember Marlene's husband, Roger, from the opening of this chapter? Well, for my husband, too, sex is at the top of his relationship intimacy list. For me, intimacy *also* involves "connecting."

(Translation = communication, which can be verbal and nonverbal.)

While dating, my Sir Ronald talked more than any other guy I'd ever met. He was constantly telling me tales of his career, exploits, family, kids, exploits, sports, travels, exploits, music, etc. His gregarious effervescence, brilliant insights, always-at-the-ready raucous laugh, and slightly off-the-wall humor captured my heart.

I grew accustomed to his repeating long stories, asking questions about my life, laughing at his own daily jokes (even those I've heard from him many times), and his expressing ongoing interest in my goals and dreams. Our tastes and goals landed us on the same page on so many levels.

As a middle-aged couple, we married about a year after meeting.

Like turning off a light switch dimmer, he stopped sharing his stories, questions, insights, goals, and humor with me. I wondered what I'd done wrong!! This jovial, brilliant man turned sullen and brooding… EXCEPT when we were out with friends.

I struggled to try and get us back on track. I missed the intellectual intimacy that had lured me. I longed for the emotional intimacy that had captured my heart.

Our physical intimacy remained strong, but I admit that I started to feel used. "He's only with me for the sex!"

I knew he loved me, but I felt hurt and distanced. And this was not something he wanted to talk about either.

Finally, it dawned on me. Nothing I had done created the distance I was sensing. He simply felt that I knew everything about him, and he knew everything about me. There was nothing more we needed to talk about, right?

Oops! I reminded him of how he'd told me that he'd felt hurt in past relationships, when they had not kept each other at the center of their focus.

The Ronald holds some strong beliefs, and he'd made himself clear from the start. For example, he does not believe a married woman should associate with male friends.

"Friends of the opposite sex must be friends with both of us," he said firmly. "We shouldn't socialize with anyone of the opposite sex *unless* you and I are *together*."

How *you* feel about the validity of his position is totally up to you. I chose to have no issue with it, though it was difficult when he expressed that he did not care to be around some of my male friends... ever.

Still, I believe we should do things to make our beloved feel secure and confident, not jealous or worried. I would never have guessed that this strong, smart, outwardly confident man housed powerful insecurities inside.

Talking about fears, insecurities, needs, wishes, concerns, dreams, and goals is something we *should* do with the person we love. These are some of the very topics and conversations that make us feel connected in the courting phase of a relationship.

We need these connections, along with those that let each other know we admire and respect them, support their dreams, are proud of their efforts, respect their time and wishes, and would marry them all over again. These *ongoing* conversations *keep* us connected.

If we are sharing challenges and concerns, laughter and life stories, dreams and dramas with someone *other* than our mate, we are making precious, intimate *connections* with someone other than our mate.

We need to keep not only physical, but emotional and intellectual connections strong and active with our beloved.

Another bit of wisdom from my honey is that the brain is our biggest sex organ. Okay. I get it. When he turns on my brain by connecting with me intellectually, I find him the sexiest man alive. I am ready to rock and roll.

We would not want the joy of physical and sexual intimacy to fade after years together. We need to also remember to keep our intellectual and emotional intimacy *every bit as sacred.*

Should we "expect" our physical, sexual, intellectual, and emotional intimacies to automatically continue throughout a marriage? Nope. At least, not in my opinion.

But I do think we should be able to expect both partners to protect and preserve the *sanctity* of these intimacies. That, to me, is part of honest loyalty.

Let's say that I am out somewhere without my husband. Maybe he had late meetings or is out of town. I may think that I am innocently sitting having a glass of wine at a bar and simply sharing stories, humor, and thoughts. However, if I am doing it with some man *other* than him, I can't help but believe that I am not only disloyal and dishonest, but I am walking a very fine cheating line.

Some might argue that point with me, but that is how I feel. I will, in fact, take it one step further.

If I *hide* this "friendship" from my spouse in *any* way, I have clearly *crossed* that line.

We never want to be taken for granted, but our partners should be able to expect our honest loyalty. That is a powerfully strong foundation block for a relationship. I want to meet the greatest expectations, without being the greatest fraud.

I want to lose 10 pounds this season.
I only have 15 to go!

Tip: Making it real starts with attitude.

15
<u>Attitude Adjustment</u>

Let your smile change the world.
Don't let the world change your smile.

Reflecting back on Marlene. Is her husband, Roger, right to "expect" his daily BJ? Or is Marlene right to think his sexual expectation makes her feel used or taken for granted?

We do not "earn" sexual intimacy any more than we can "earn" emotional or intellectual intimacy.

If something physical happened to our partner that prevented them from sharing sexual intimacy, we would not blame them nor feel they were withholding their love.

I can't help but think that a little communication could help them both feel appreciated and satisfied. For instance, Roger may have thought that his words were a playful way to hint to Marlene that he really liked her "attentions," and he missed them on days when that connection was missing. However, Marlene interpreted Roger's words very differently and felt hurt, belittled, and used.

We are human, and we often speak before thinking, especially with people with whom we are very familiar, such as our closest loved ones.

Way too often, we fail to show consideration, thoughtfulness, and respect. Unfortunately, we all know that we should be gratefully aware of every sweet word and loving action... as if they were gifts.

This reminds me of a wonderful book I read, entitled "Silver Boxes," by Florence Littauer. I had the good fortune to meet her and her husband, Fred, many years ago.

She truly is the encourager she encourages others to be. Her book brims with charming examples of how important it is to present our words as if they were precious gifts.

How many of us recognize the power we hold in our words and the importance of thoughtfully delivering them to a listener as precious gifts, all wrapped up in silver boxes and bows? I contend that we do even better when we serve up our attitude and actions the same way.

I'm not weird.
I'm a limited edition.

* * * * * * * * * * *

Robert complained that Ginny was way too bitchy. She seemed to always be cross with him. He was tired of walking on eggshells around her, regularly anticipating her next complaint or nagging demand.

"She doesn't *ask* me to do anything," he explained. "She *demands* it… loudly and meanly, as if I was her most-hated servant."

This was most difficult to hear, because Ginny consistently comes across very sweetly with us. Of course, as with all of us, we only see her public side… the qualities and characteristics she chooses to show us. Robert sees her private side.

She's not alone with the challenge of failing to exercise the same polite or respectful discipline with the very person who loves her the most.

For Robert's part, it was killing him emotionally to feel beaten down by Ginny daily. We know she loves her husband very much and would never deliberately behave in a manner that would hurt him.

In fact, in speaking with Ginny, I learned that she was frustrated with herself. She truly had been a very sweet person with Robert… for years.

He had been the crabby, demanding partner. She never felt as if she could do anything right in his eyes, no matter how hard she tried to please him.

Ginny had given up and then given in. She started fighting with him, going toe-to-toe in mental jousting almost daily. She admitted that somehow Robert had gotten his act together and stopped barking at her. But he'd also stopped doing anything around the house.

She felt overburdened with her work and their home. Ginny certainly did not want to hurt him, but she wanted a husband and partner, not a do-nothing roommate.

Out in public, we rarely show negative undercurrents that may be running through our lives. And, in private, few of us have the courage to talk openly with our partners about personal challenges. We seem to think that, somehow, things will just magically get better.

The person we marry is our best friend, but we forget to treat them that way sometimes. For Ginny and Robert, both needed an attitude adjustment. They pledged to be kinder to each other and to show more respect for each other and each other's time and feelings. He vowed to stop being a couch potato while she handled all the household chores alone. She promised to ask and not demand, recognizing that "no" *is* a legitimate answer sometimes.

I share their story with you because we may all find ourselves in different places at various times in our lives. We are imperfect humans and are bound to need attitude adjustments from time to time.

It's just a bad day, not a bad life.

To me, Step 1 is developing and then maintaining an "Attitude of Gratitude." That's an old expression, but it can breathe new life into a relationship.

Think for a moment about all the things you have. Your list might include good health, a job, a loving spouse, a home, a car that runs, great friends, healthy children, living parents, strong faith, and so on. Think simply when making your list.

Perhaps people tell you what a wonderful smile you have, a great laugh or sense of humor. Maybe you have some special talents, such as playing a sport or a musical instrument, singing, dancing, cooking, growing flowers, solving math problems, or even crossword puzzles.

We tend to be hard on ourselves. When we get "down" or feel "low," it becomes more difficult to see joy in anything.

Create that list of things that are good in your life. Read your "I Am Grateful" list daily, if need be, and add to it regularly.

A good attitude becomes easier to maintain when we sincerely feel grateful for the bounty we actually do have.

A *great* attitude comes when we make a habit out of having a *good* attitude.

Tip: Life usually gives us another chance. It's called "Tomorrow."

Sometimes I write down tasks that I have completed...
just to get the satisfaction of crossing them off my To Do list.

16
Avoid the "Stresspools" of Life

No one needs to be around someone who dulls the shine on a brand new penny.

Whether we know it or choose to admit it, we are either an Encourager or a Discourager. We each make a choice as to which type we will be… every day. Discouragers bring "stresspools."

I call any of those places that add unnecessary stress and aggravation "stresspools." They are just as stinky and rotten as cesspools, but "stresspools" wreak of tension, strain, anxiety, worry, hassle, pressure, and emotional trauma.

Sometimes we unwittingly fling ourselves into these pits of grief. Usually, however, we get knocked in by people around us.

One husband had been nagging his wife to clean up some clutter that had been gathering in the basement. She knew they needed to get through a lot of "stuff" that had gathered from themselves and their now adult children over the 20 years they'd lived in the house.

This was not an afternoon project, or even one for a couple of weekends. It would take many days of work.

Still, just a couple or hours later, she gleefully announced that she had already filled their huge trash and recycle barrels. She knew he'd be so pleased that she'd started on the massive project.

Instead he snapped, "Hmph! I should have gotten a dumpster. You need to throw that much away."

"Okay, you're welcome, dear," she must have thought.

An Encourager might have said, "That's great. You've made a wonderful start today. Thank you!"

A Discourager chooses a path that's more like, "Well, big deal. You have a long way to go." Or, "You should have done it months ago."

Give an optimist a bowl of lemons; she will make lemonade. Give a pessimist a bowl of lemons; he will throw them at people.

We've all heard advice to avoid negative people. There's scientific evidence to back that up. As humans, we tend to be hyper-sensitive, especially to personal criticism.

Think back to some point in a school or work scenario when several people greeted you with positive tones and comments about how great you look today or about what a great job you did on that last project.

Then one person comes along and asks if you are feeling all right today. You say, "Yeah, sure. Why?"

They respond with something like, "Oh, I don't know. You just look at little tired, and don't seem like your usual self. I thought you might be coming down with the flu or something."

Instantly, we forget about all the positive support we got before this one negative comment. We scurry off to a mirror to see if we look sick. One negative comment can wipe out 20 positive ones.

Another tough behavior we want to avoid is nagging or harping on something. Yet, many people nag and harp on their loved ones, especially at home or in private.

I'll bet they wouldn't do that at work. Think about it. No one ever earned a pay raise or got a promotion by nagging their boss.

I believe there is more than one "right" way to get things done. However, if someone negatively harps on me about something *they* want done, that's the best way to find me digging in my heels and not doing it... my way *or* their way.

I am stubborn, but I also know that if I do the task after being bitched out at high speed... over and over... it will encourage this bad behavior to be repeated. Hell, no!

If I do what is asked under such circumstances, it's only to hush the crabbiness. Period.

Mom always told me that if I couldn't say something nice,
then I shouldn't say anything at all.
Still, some people wonder why I'm so quiet around them.

Control Freaks are also important types to avoid, as they bring "stresspools" wherever they go. They don't make it easy, because, as we talked about earlier, Control Freaks usually don't see it in themselves.

Again, Control Freaks frequently point at others in their lives – their spouses, business partners, associates, or even their children – and try to loudly and frequently label *them* as Control Freaks. They seriously don't understand that all those same people recognize the truth, despite the CF's verbal protests to the contrary.

Try to find some balance. Real discussions happen when all opinions are validated and welcomed, even if you don't agree with each other.

If anything less is happening in your relationship, someone is unfairly demanding all the control... all the power.

Imagine being in a brainstorming session, where the basic premise is that there is no place for criticism or belittling of another person's ideas, input, or opinions. Every idea gets to go on the table. All thoughts and possibilities are genuinely welcomed. If you think something said is silly, fine. *You* also have a right to say things *they* may find silly. Once all ideas are shared, you can better discuss the merits, challenges, and possibilities of each.

I am also a great believer in not pushing each other's "buttons" just because we know where they are! That's part of trusting each other. We need to trust that our vulnerabilities and challenges are safe with the person we love.

I'd also rather do things for someone with joy in my heart… to make them happy… and *not* because they commanded it or ranted and raved.

Now, I don't like "stuff" being repeatedly dumped on the kitchen counter. It tends to collect there for days on end… unopened mail, gloves, keys, paperwork, hats, miscellaneous tools, notes, gadgets, magazines, electronics, etc. My husband also hates this, though he inadvertently does this himself with great regularity.

One day he blew up, yelling for me to get my stuff off the counter, or he was going to throw it all away. I calmly said, "Okay." I got up from the table, walked to the counter, picked up the sunglasses I had placed there, and sat back down with him at the kitchen table.

Initially, Sir Ronald glared at me, as if I was being defiant, rather than compliant. I calmly stated, "All the remaining items and piles are not mine."

He rather sheepishly looked toward the mess. He then looked back at me and sternly stated, "Well, keep it that way."

We then both burst out laughing.

It's easy to see things that are out of place as unnecessary junk, especially when these things belong to someone else. This "stuff" has little or no value to us. However, part of respecting someone else is respecting the things that are important to them.

I also try to not "bug" my honey. I have been called many things throughout my life, but "bitch" was never one of them. I make it a point to not nag. I will ask once. I may even remind once. If the task remains undone, I can choose to do it myself or let it go.

I have learned to live with someone else's projects that they started, yet did not finish, sometimes for years.

One of the most important choices I made was to not let such things upset me or become stresspools.

Learning to roll with the punches reduces our stress. I came to a realization decades ago. In an adult family scenario, I am only in charge of me. I must decide if I will or won't let actions of other people upset me, because I am not interested in stressing myself out trying to get others to live "my" way.

For example, I love to cook. Toward that end, I enjoy large "lazy Susan" rotating shelves of herbs and spices at eye level. For simplicity, I alphabetize them.

Often, others pull various bottles off those shelves and put them back in all different places. I could get upset and try explaining to them… again… that I'd like labels facing forward, and bottles arranged alphabetically. Okay. I do that once. Period. Then, I simply take the time to arrange them back in order as needed.

No one is hassled. No one is upset. I am not putting a "stresspool" in someone else's life. My silly alphabetized herbs system is only important to me.

I try to apply that calm in other areas, too. I offer to help once or twice. Then I genuinely let it go.

So, I can choose to look past the entertainment console that remains pulled out away from the wall with wires dangling… for several weeks or even several months at a time. I decide not to be annoyed at the big hole dug beside the wall in a side garden where Hubby has been saying he is putting in a fountain… for three years. I look past the piles of magazines and paperwork that he has kept randomly stacked in our office… for months on end. I ignore the sharp coloration difference in the barn roof with one quarter of the cedar shakes re-stained… almost four years ago. I close the door if an adult child who has moved back in with us keeps their room in total disarray… always.

Smile… It confuses people.

No one else "makes" us do anything. They can't make us nag them, or make us angry, or make us have to strike out at them, or make us drink alcohol, or make us yell at them, or anything else. We are responsible for our choices, including our responses and reactions.

If there were past misdeeds, I do not believe we should nag or repeat them, never mind throw them in someone's face. If they sincerely apologized and we genuinely forgave them, we must move on. Learn from mistakes, but move on. If we bring them up and toss them at the offender, we may *not* have actually forgiven them, even if we claim we have.

Past misdeeds must only serve as a reference point in calm conversation about lessons learned or actions that taught us to behave better. They should never be bantered about with sarcasm, anger, or nastiness.

Tip: No one needs to dip even one toe in any "stresspool."

Section 5
BIG LITTLE DIFFERENCES

17
Man versus Woman

"I do not think I ever opened a book in my life which had not something to say about women's inconstancy. Songs and proverbs all talk of woman's fickleness. But perhaps you will note, these were all written by men."
- Jane Austen (1775 – 1817)
English novelist in "Persuasion"

*"Do you really believe that everything
historians tell us about men or about women is actually true?
You ought to consider the fact
that these histories have been written by men,
who never tell the truth except by accident."*
- Moderata Fonte (Modesta di Pozzo di Forzi) (1555 – 1592)
Italian writer in "The Worth of Women: Wherein Is Clearly
Revealed Their Nobility and Their Superiority to Men"

*"If women are so flighty, fickle, changeable, susceptible, and inconstant,
as some would have us believe,
why must their suitors resort to such trickery
to have their way with them?
There is no need to go to war for a castle that is already captured."*
-Christine de Pizan (1364 – 1430)
French author in "Der Sendbrief vom Liebesgott /
The Letter of the God of Love"

*"Wine and women make wise men dote and forsake God's law
and do wrong.
However, the fault is not in the wine and often not in the woman.
The fault is in the one who misuses the wine or the woman."*
- Anonymous

When Help Is Helpless

I just love reading some marriage therapist rambling on and on about how a woman must tell her man how much she appreciates all he does for her and avoid making requests in a negative, unappreciative or demanding tone. Or else she opens the door to "another woman" stepping in and filling this basic, yet important need. She may be a social friend or a co-worker, but she is a woman who addresses him nicely and always showers him with appreciation for everything he does.

Hello! Appreciation and respect are *mutual* needs.

Any relationship gurus worth their salts address the needs of and with *both* partners. Seriously. If a man fails to appreciate all a woman does for *him*, their families, and their home, then *she* feels used and taken for granted, too. If he compounds this by making requests that sound like demands or commands or speaks to her in a negative, unappreciative, demeaning, or demanding tone, he also opens the door for "another man" to fill her important basic need for appreciation and respect.

As vulnerable as an unappreciated man may be to his co-worker or a new chum at a bar, so is an unappreciated woman vulnerable to her co-worker or a new chum at a bar.

We may be wired differently as men and women, but some needs are parallel human needs.

Julie, a new advertising associate, arrived home bursting with excitement to tell her husband, John, how well her big presentation had gone. She'd not only landed a major account, but the leadership team had rewarded her with a nice promotion and pay raise.

He wasn't home yet, so she realized he must have stopped at one of his favorite haunts for a drink. She wished he'd called her so she could have joined him, but he tended to forget to do that.

Regardless, she gleefully set about preparing a celebratory dinner and chilled the bottle of champagne she'd picked up to add festivity to her news.

When she heard his car door, Julie scurried to greet him at the door with the bottle and two glasses in hand. As he came in, she gave him a welcome home kiss along with a big smile.

"What's with the champagne?" John asked, moving past her toward the kitchen.

"I have some wonderful news," Julie bubbled.

"Just give me a minute to relax," he replied.

"Oh. Based on the time, I thought you must have already relaxed somewhere for Happy Hour," she said. "I wish you'd have called. I would have gladly joined you."

"Whatever," John said. "It was just the usual crowd. Okay. Okay. What's your news?"

"I rocked the presentation, got the account, AND a $10,000 pay raise!" Julie sparkled, holding up the champagne, "Shall I pour, or would you like to do the honors?"

"That's great, but I really don't feel like champagne tonight. Maybe we could just eat a little dinner and watch some television." John walked into the family room and stretched out on the sofa, turning on the TV with the remote control.

Okayyyy. Julie stood there… crushed.

Was it really so difficult to be happy for her? She worked longer hours than he did and never complained.

She would never dream of going out to Happy Hour without inviting him. And she tried hard not to resent him for simply assuming that he could do as he pleased, while she'd be the "good little wife" and rush home to prepare dinner for him.

A little reciprocal respect and appreciation would certainly be nice. This, for her, was big! HUGE!

Here she'd made this exciting announcement, including the biggest pay raise she'd ever gotten, and he'd responded as if she'd told him that she'd brought in the mail.

Knowingly or not, John had just slammed her. He was the one she'd wanted to rush home to, to share her excitement and success with in celebration. He'd crushed her like an unwanted bit of cracker.

Time is often all that separates love from hatred.

How often will Julie be likely to dare open up and share her heart and dreams with John in the future? She risks being crushed again or tossed aside… by the most important person to her.

Okay. If this was a one-time occurrence, or if he'd had something heavy-duty on his mind, she might understand and not even feel as hurt. However, if this was part of a pattern, he may soon find himself making up excuses for why their marriage didn't work out.

Julie's steadfast good nature, work ethic, and positive attitude make her a very attractive catch for someone who *does* recognize, respect, and appreciate her efforts and skill.

Don't think for a moment that Julie's story is far-fetched. Hopefully it does not mirror anything in your own life. However, stories of miscommunication and lack of appreciation and respect abound.

Love is blind. Marriage can open your eyes.

How We Can Do Better

We all benefit if we look at anything a loved one does to help out as a gift. Maybe they got a raise, like Julie did.

If we *don't* celebrate their successes with them, why wouldn't they feel the need to start hanging around people who *do* show appreciation and give them a few "atta-boys" and well-deserved pats on the back?

The one we love may have done something simple, something they may regularly do… cooked a great meal, took out the trash, washed your car, fixed something that was broken, cleaned out the cat's litter box, wiped down the shower, picked up things that had been left around the house, made the bed, put away laundry, or mowed the lawn.

Be sure to sincerely say, "Thank you" to them at least once each and every day. A little appreciation goes a very long way.

* * * * * * * * * * * *

I like the sound of you not talking.

Mark loved his wife, and he believed that she loved him, too. However, Sharon's negative tones, sarcastic responses, and hateful looks told him that if they didn't find a way to get back onto a better communication track, their relationship could be heading for a dead end.

"Sharon," he started. "I love you very much. I am concerned with the negative tones our conversations have taken on and would like us to work together to start communicating more positively."

Nicely done. He did not point fingers. He used a positive, constructive tone. He expressed his love and desire to work together as a team. Still, Sharon was on the defensive.

"Oh, really!?!" She continued, "We spent $60,000 on getting you a master's degree in communication, and you are the absolute worst communicator in the world!"

Mark resisted the urge to reply negatively in kind, though it was extremely tempting to throw a verbal slam into the ring. Instead, he simply said that he hoped that they could both work together to do better, because he believed in their marriage and felt that they could be happier together and feel more loved if they communicated better.

He asked her to consider it, to just think about it.

Yet, Sharon went off on him rampantly, and he knew it was not a good time for a conversation. She had decided that he was 100% wrong.

In reality, it was she who yelled, overreacted, twisted scenarios in a failed attempt to make him out to be the villain, and held back any semblance of loving words to him.

It matters not which partner is bringing negativity into conversations and exchanges. Toxicity has no place at all between people who have promised to love each other.

The Fix

I believe the cure starts with one partner doing exactly what Mark did. Step back and make the decision to speak with your loved one in calm, supportive, loving, appreciative, and respectful tones, looks, and words.

Though the response may well be habitually negative, doing the right thing in tough circumstances is an important part of showing unconditional love.

For more great concepts on "the fix," check out the companion book to this one, "The Golf Pro Has Heart." Author John A. Gehrisch reveals what I call "secrets that have been hiding in plain sight" in the JAG Formula for happy, loving, long-term relationships.

A major component is getting two "Giver" personalities together. He also emphasizes our vital concepts of respect, support, and appreciation in a loving relationship.

If you can't get someone out of your head,
then maybe they're supposed to be there.

Let me wrap up this chapter with a touch of humor, rather than a tip. This gem was shared by a friend who knows I have a sense of humor and could "take it."

****

"I just got off the phone with friend living in North Dakota near the Canadian border. He said that since early this morning the snow has been nearly waist high and is still falling. The temperature is dropping way below zero and the north wind is increasing to near gale force. His wife has done nothing but look through the kitchen window and just stare. He says that if it gets much worse, he may have to let her in."

18
Created Equal but Different

Wherever you find a great man,
you will find a great mother or a great wife
standing behind him –
or so they used to say.
It would be interesting to know how many great women
have had great fathers and husbands behind them.
– Dorothy L. Sayers (1893 – 1957)
English writer in "Gaudy Night"

Vive la Différence

We can complement each other because of our differences. We can complete each other because of our differences.

We can both enjoy a sense of rivalry, but science tells us that men will want to dominate and be more aggressive in addressing conflict.

I am not at all sure that is an accurate "blanket" statement any more than any other stereotype. I have known some extraordinarily aggressive women, as well as some men who are astutely talented in mediation and thoughtful compromise.

Consider any of the truly inaccurate generalizations you've heard over the years. Real men don't each quiche. Men hate cats. Women are complicated. Women are mysterious to men.

It seems that we humans come up with overgeneralizations frequently. Perhaps we do it whenever <u>we</u> don't understand a person or people. Or we want to feel more comfortable.

We're back to attitude. We each choose how we react or respond to everything that happens to us or around us, to whatever is said, to whatever we read, and to everything we see.

So, we could choose to celebrate our differences, rather than over-analyze them. This might help us become more realistic about the generalizations to which we subscribe.

For example, consider this. If women are the overemotional ones, why do so many bar fights break out between men? Such brawls do not spring from logical, calm places.

Hollywood Style

Consider films we often call "chick flicks" versus those we dub as "bro films." Both genres tend to have story lines that follow pretty basic formulas for storytelling and success.

Chick flicks are not only romantic comedies, sappy musicals, or fairytales. They are comedies and dramas, often filled with courtship, genuine love, and family relationships, with emphasis on the human experience through relationships, with both laughter and tears. They're often teen-oriented films. They usually have drama and heartache in the script, sometimes even a final tragedy that must be endured. Some cross over from suspense. They often feature strong female characters, regardless of age.

Bro films likely feature less complex storylines, though plenty of tension and drama. They include wild westerns, war films, and save-the-world-from-disaster plots. They will likely have fast cars, faster women, explosions, blood, crimes, sex, adventures, bad guys, and plenty of swearing. Oh, *and* we should be ready for a more than healthy dose of fighting, whether with weapons or fists.

Both types actually have heroes we can cheer. They rise up from a serious underdog position. Both have villains and challenges to be overcome against great odds. Both can be drama or comedy, history or suspense.

In truth, a variety of "bro films" are plenty sappy enough to land in the category of "chick flicks." And some powerfully strong "story" scripts have violence and action aplenty.

"If we look to history, we shall find that women who have distinguished themselves have neither been the most beautiful nor the most gentle of their sex."

– Mary Wollstonecraft (1759 – 1797)
English writer and philosopher
in "A Vindication of the Rights of Women"

*"What we ask is to be human individuals,
however peculiar and unexpected.
It is no good saying:
'You are a little girl and therefore you ought to like dolls.'
If the answer is, 'But I don't,' there is no more to be said."*

– Dorothy L. Sayers (1893 – 1957)
English writer in "Are Women Human?
Astute and Witty Essays on the Role of Women in Society"

Reality Check

If everything and everybody on this planet matched with perfect sameness, it sure would be boring. Men and women are different, and we always will be. Recognizing differences is important. That does not make one thing better or worse than another.

I'm not crazy. My reality is just different than yours.

When it comes to people… you could aptly say that I am a racist… a *human* racist. I believe in *people*. There are good and not-so-good people of all colors and creeds. I'm not here to judge. Period.

As people, we draw judgments from others when we *behave* badly, especially when we try to blame our bad behavior on others. This is not based on race, age, sex, or religion. It's based on behavior differences.

We have no problem appreciating differences in foods we eat. You may like a certain food, but not like a particular preparation. For example, what if you like fish, but you don't like it fried? It doesn't mean you are putting down fish in general; you just don't personally care for it fried. No big deal.

It's like when I'd review theatre for the television news. I once had a news director who loved it when I'd really pan a show. He wanted to see me rip up more theatre companies… *all* theatre companies. I looked at him as though he was from another planet.

I'd only give a wretchedly negative review to a company touting itself as professional or a Broadway bound Actors Equity union theatre that EARNED the bad review.

I was certainly NOT going to lambaste some high-spirited community theatre or a college troupe at a school that didn't even have a drama *class*, never mind an acting *major*.

Different is a proper distinction. It's called integrity. Duh.

R-E-S-P-E-C-T

Some people feel the rain. Others just get wet.

I do think that some people need to work harder than others to earn respect. Often it's because of others' perceptions.

For example, someone might look sweet and gentle, but the job may call for firm and tough. Stereotypes regarding attractive women often come into play here. A woman (or a man) may be very likeable.

However, if the woman "talks tough" she is criticized as abrasive and bitchy. A man saying the same words in the same tones is typically viewed as strong and credible.

Society seems to want a successful woman to appear relaxed, trim and sexy while needing to behave like a "strong woman." That's a tough tight-rope to walk. Inner strength needs to grow and grow, without losing spirit during an uphill battle.

These role expectations play out in our personal relationships, as well. We can spotlight the many double standards in our "equal but different" reality. For example, even in this day in age, many people frown on a woman stepping out to a bar for a drink... alone. Yet, for a man, the same exact action is seen as perfectly acceptable.

Or consider a woman learning some heart-breaking news. It's commonly considered fine if tears roll down her cheeks. Yet for a man, the same exact reaction can be viewed as weak and inappropriate.

> *My husband thinks I'm crazy.*
> *However, he's the one who married me.*

Sandra and Sean had reached an impasse. He was hiding what he did when she was not around. He'd go out to bars where he did not take her. He'd meet women and present himself to them as single, available, and interested. He'd collect names and numbers and follow-up with these other women to try and meet them out again.

When a friend, Peter, saw Sean in one of these bars, acting inappropriately, he spoke to Sean about it. Sean initially tried to say it was the first time it had happened and that it wouldn't happen again.

A couple months later, he got caught... again. Peter took him aside and said, "Sean, this is not right. What about Sandra?"

"Don't *you* worry about Sandra. She is fine," Sean shot back.

This time, Peter did what I believe is a strong act of friendship. He said, "Okay. I will give you complete control here. *You* decide which one of us tells her."

That got Sean really ticked off. *"You* keep *out* of this," he ordered his friend.

"No," Peter said simply. "You are both friends of mine. I will not be put in the middle because of *your* bad behavior. I won't be seeing you guys until Saturday, so you have three days to come clean. And I don't mean come up with excuses. On Saturday, I will expect you to bring this up to me in front of Sandra. Or I will."

Sandra is a strong lady. She is classy all the way. While no relationship is perfect, Sean admits that she treats him wonderfully, and he'd marry her again in a heartbeat. With no marital problems, why does Sean have the need to get "built up" by other women? · He didn't know.

However, several friends in addition to Peter had decided that much of his loud and boisterous social persona… and regular flirting with other women… were signs of great insecurity. He loved presenting himself as strong, confident, and independent. Yet, he was very weak in ways that deeply hurt his wife and marriage.

It takes a strong woman to tolerate a weak man. That said, it takes a strong man to tolerate a weak woman, too. These scenarios are by no means exclusive to men. The strength to which I refer is internal… guts… fortitude… heart… soul.

Physical strength is different. Based on typical size differences, men tend to be far stronger physically.

That kind of strength is very easy to abuse. We especially see this with internally weak men intimidating or beating on people who are physically weaker.

> *"Oh, it is excellent to have a giant's strength,*
> *but it is tyrannous to use it like a giant."*
> -- William Shakespeare (1564 – 1616)
> English poet and playwright in "Measure for Measure"

Getting Stronger

I think we need to develop a powerful dose of tolerance to understand each other's humanness. None of us is perfect. It's not only okay that we are different; it's actually great. This is why we can find "completion" in our partner.

My husband gets very excited talking about car engines and technical details. That bores me to tears. He can watch sports... almost any sports... for hours on end.

I like sports, but certainly not in the portions he enjoys. However, just because he has some stereotypically male interest areas does not make it wrong.

On the other hand, I lack some of the stereotypically female interest areas. I couldn't care less about going to chick flics or out to lunch to gossip with "the girls."

And I avoid going shopping at a mall (or anywhere else) like the plague. Failing to meet some stereotypically female interest areas is neither right nor wrong. It's simply a matter of personal taste.

My husband loves to shop, likes large floral prints and is a good cook. These are stereotypically female interests. I like the color blue, am a very good driver, and I have wonderful spatial sense... all on the list of male stereotypes.

Of course, we both have LOTS of traits and interests that <u>do</u> come from the stereotype lists for our own sex.

So what? Stereotypes don't apply to everyone. Our differences make us stronger. We complement each other.

It only becomes sad in societies that do not *let*, never mind *encourage*, both sexes to rise to their own full potential, whether typical or not.

It is hard to believe sometimes that nations still exist where men insist on complete domination of women.

To maintain this edge, they vehemently protest and prevent the education of women, and take steps to keep women from learning about cultures or having free say in their own futures or even their daily activities.

In these cultures, careers for women are almost nonexistent. Such oppression is brutal in any form and holds back these entire societies. I can only imagine that future generations will consider us to have been barbaric for our intolerance of differences.

Tip: Celebrate being human and alive.

19
Dastardly Double Standards

*"When a man gives his opinion, he's a man.
When a woman gives her opinion, she's a bitch."*
-- Bette Davis (1908 – 1989)
American actress

Double standards exist in many arenas, from race and religion to sex and age. We are looking at relationships and sexual double standards. These double standards quite simply exist when one set of rules or principles gets applied to men and another set for the same conditions gets applied to women. They abound.

A man is applauded and called a stud for having successfully dated many women. A woman who has dated many men is called promiscuous and a slut.

As we learned in Frank Loesser's song, "Luck Be a Lady" in the musical "Guys and Dolls," we can't expect luck or love to be either fair or nice. This also applies to Life and double standards. They're not always fair, and they're not always nice.

Young girls can wear their hair long to school. Young boys are often told to get a haircut.

Women should be sexually submissive. Men need not.

You should busy yourself cleaning the house and cooking, though your partner lounges in bed or on the sofa watching television reruns.

If our first sexual intercourse experience was had at a young age in an uncommitted relationship, public reaction to males is more positive than to females.

Men are seen as sexy though sporting hairy armpits and legs. Women doing the same are seen as "feminazis."

You mustn't see your men friends, but *he* can keep contact with his gal pals.

Men can be seen in public or in photographs without their shirts, but a photo of a woman breastfeeding her baby gets banned.

You will go to jail for raising a hand to her, but *she* can beat on you without legal consequence.

If a man and woman share a light kiss good-bye in public, it is generally okay. If a gay or lesbian couple does the same, it is usually frowned upon.

Sexual acts between women are considered "hot." Sexual acts between men are not.

He is deemed as handsome and desirable if his hair turns gray, but she is called unattractive and matronly if she doesn't "wash away" that gray.

You should not do this and never do that. Yet, your spouse keeps doing it.

A single man in his 40's or 50's is viewed as an eligible bachelor. A single woman in her 40's or 50's is viewed as an Old Maid or damaged goods.

A man who speaks his mind at a meeting is viewed as having leadership skills. A woman doing the same is seen as bossy and pushy.

Men in action film roles are quite often bloody, dirty, and gross looking. Women in action film roles are quite often sexy, dressed in tight clothing, and sport perfect hair and make-up.

It's okay for men to be "lounge lizards" and out "on the prowl." Women are frowned at for going out looking for "action."

Double standards only work for the person applying them. The recipient is merely suffering the brunt of unfairness.

If the situations were reversed, perhaps that offending person would start to understand, because they certainly wouldn't like having it done to them.

Double standards get applied in a wide variety of facets in life. They can be financial, behavioral, and sexual.

* * * * * * * * * * *

Ann needed to spend three days away to pay a quick visit with her aging parents about 1,000 miles away. Her husband, Charles, was also invited, but he said that the cost of the extra $99 ticket meant he needed to stay home.

Then, as he drove her to the airport, Charles added that Ann should not take her parents out at all. "We need to *not* spend money going out right now." Okay. No problem.

When Ann got back home, she learned that her husband had gone out to three different bars and restaurants on *each* of the three nights she was gone! Charles had dropped more than $100 each and every night on something *she* was asked not to do.

Further, Ann then learned from friends that when people asked Charles where she was, her husband had literally told them that he had no idea! Poor baby.

Needless to say, Ann was not impressed with his shenanigans. One of the people who "ratted him out" turned out to be a single woman that he'd entertained in his wife's absence. He'd tried to present himself as a poor victim of a roving wife. Thankfully, she was not buying his contrived "plight."

Some couples do go out to bars and restaurants independent of each other. Others choose to only go out with each other. This needs to be established mutually in each relationship.

Double standards definitely should not come into play in this area. If he wants to do a "Boys Night Out" occasionally or regularly, she should also feel comfortable with equal opportunities for a "Girls Night Out."

Girls Night Out / Boys Night Out

Some women enjoy getting together for shopping or lunch or other such activities, just as some men enjoy getting together to watch a sporting event or do some mechanical work or something. There's absolutely nothing wrong with this; it's very healthy for those who like to do this.

Now, brace yourself. To keep it healthy and positive try not to forget a basic: No alcohol in mixed company.

"WHAT?!!?" You may ask. Keep in mind, you're on a *Boys* Night Out or a *Girls* Night Out. Once we start drinking in mixed company, the game is over. Now it's a Night Out *without* our lover. We've broken the rules. Have drinks, but do it with just the boys or just the girls. Watch the game at someone's house and have all the drinks you want. Enjoy our sidewalk café luncheon with cocktails.

Just don't move the group into a bar or club setting where we are socializing with both men and women. If we are socializing in mixed company, then we should have our spouse with us.

In the vast majority of bar settings, if we remove the couples from the picture, we are pretty much left with married men and prowling women or married women and prowling men. These are not gentlemen; these are not ladies.

It's no joke when they tell women that if they want to meet a married man just go to a singles bar or join an online dating service.

It is sad how deeply buried even the thought of integrity is in our modern day cavemen.

Actually, I misuse the term "men." Those are still just boys, disguising themselves in adult bodies.

Now, to get to the bottom line… If you are comfortable in the bar setting with mixed company, at least be sure that you are not socializing with the opposite sex. This should be obvious.

If we socialize in mixed company we are not being kind, and perhaps not respectful nor truthful with our spouse or ourselves. It's bogus. We need to stop kidding ourselves. It is most important to not put our important personal relationship in a disrespectful light, at best… and in jeopardy of compromise, at worst.

Woman's Work

"A woman's work is never done." So the saying goes. Hmmmm… A good ***person's*** work is never done.

The old adage referred to traditionally female household duties that require repetition… making beds, washing dishes, bathing babies, cooking meals, doing laundry, cleaning up after meals, doing marketing, budgeting, cleaning rooms, raising children, loving a spouse, volunteering in a community and church, and more. These are tasks often handled by both men and women today.

It Is Written

There's no news flash when we recognize that many double standards between men and women may not have been openly discussed, especially in the past, but they have been shared in novels and writings. This is especially true when we look at some writing by women early in the 20th Century and in earlier times.

"As long as she thinks of a man, nobody objects to a woman thinking."
-- Virginia Woolf (1882 – 1941)
English author in *"Orlando"*

"I have never been able to find out precisely what feminism is. I only know that people call me a feminist whenever I express sentiments that differentiate me from a doormat... or a prostitute."

-- Rebecca West (1892-1983)
English author in *"Young Rebecca, Writings"*

"The rule seemed to be that a great woman must either die unwed or find a still greater man to marry her. The great man, on the other hand, could marry where he liked, not being restricted to great women. Indeed, it was often found sweet and commendable in him to choose a woman of no sort of greatness at all"

-- Dorothy L. Sayers (1893 – 1957)
English writer in *"Gaudy Night"*

Evolve or Dissolve…Double Trouble

We are in a constant state of change. That's just part of who we are, although people tend to resist change. However, movement of the human race is never lateral. We either progress or regress, depending on our personal choices within societal mores.

This is not particular to this era, but it has always been so. For example, during the Roman Empire, adultery was illegal. However, it was tolerated for married men, but not women.

If a woman cheated on her husband, he not only divorced her, but he could tie her outside the house for a period of three days to subject her to public ridicule while announcing what she had done. She then could be exiled to an island… an island other than the one to which her extramarital lover was sent.

And THAT was considered a modern civilization.

Move forward a couple of thousand years, and advanced societies would never consider such behavior to be just nor acceptable.

That is NOT to say that we don't still have a lot of ludicrous double standards, such as those we've listed in this chapter.

The ridiculousness of our sexual double standards is very clear. Most of us know at least one someone who loves to "check out" people they find attractive. These same "someones" typically admit that they would never stand for such behavior from their own spouse or partner.

Here's another one. I have heard a number of men say that they would not want to date a woman with children. Okay, but some of these men have children themselves. They expect a woman to accept and be nurturing for their children, but these particular men do not want the "hassle" of dealing with the children of some other male. I guess that's better than some species in which a male will kill and even eat the offspring of another male.

I happen to believe that single parents, both male and female, should focus on their children and separate their dating life from their children. Kids don't benefit from meeting a revolving door of dates. However, once a relationship becomes serious and committed, I think it's time to involve the children. A healthy, loving relationship is one of the most positive role model examples adults can set for children.

We humans may recognize that we have dastardly double standard problems, but we sometimes must admit that we are too weak to shape up.

Tip: We've still got a long way to evolve, so we should try to step forward a little every day.

20

Failure to Communicate and Then Some

When we start dating someone, it seems to be in our human nature to put our best foot forward. After the wedding, it becomes easy to slip into some lazy patterns that become habits.

She may make snide remarks. He starts presuming she knows what he's thinking. She gives him an evil "look." He doesn't even bother to chat, never mind talk to her. They both resort to nasty name calling.

They may truly love each other, but they have completely forgotten to *ever* put their best foot forward for each other. Initially this may seem a natural phase in the relationship, but it's a good phase to skip or move through as quickly as possible. Otherwise, little superficial glimpses of unloving behavior can swell into huge problems.

Often a negative partner does not realize exactly *how* negative they are. In fact, they frequently point the accusing finger at their spouse. If you've experienced this, you know exactly what I mean.

Numerous studies back up the fact that, usually, when one partner in a relationship starts making odd claims or statements, they are merely transferring their issues to their spouse. What they "charge" their spouse with is the very thing that they themselves are doing.

They may be becoming secretive and devious.

When it comes to sex, she may start "holding out" or start claiming that *he* holds out.

When it comes to trust, he may start telling folks that <u>he</u> can't trust *her*, and this is actually because *he* is untrustworthy.

If you suggest that you both try counseling, your spouse may make it very clear that it is YOU who needs help, not HIM.

Often a spouse may try to play the "blame game." They may charge that "YOU always do this."

A healthier approach is to say that I feel hurt, neglected, alone, or let down, when this or that happens.

When it comes to privacy and secrecy, he may observe that she used to ask him to answer her cell phone when it was near him. Now she screams for him to not touch it.

He goes out without her and starts charging these "excursions" on new, non-joint credit cards with statements she will not ever see.

Sometimes, couples simply stop talking… at least with each other. Now I've heard all those scientific study results about how many thousands of words per day are spoken by the average female, versus the far fewer thousands of words per day uttered by the average male. And I know some talkative females. (I am most assuredly one of them.) On the other hand, I know some verbose men who can outtalk even the chattiest of women.

Sometimes I wish my mouth had a "Backspace" key…

To me, it is sad when couples *stop* talking. If we go silent on our partner, we are literally eliminating one of our most beloved methods of foreplay! Remember, we *talked* with our partners first. We'll get into more detail on this later.

Some people, both men and women, do not like to talk and never have. Others do most of their talking when in groups or out in public. Some only like to converse in quiet or even private, low-keyed scenarios. We are all different.

I, for one, grew up with lots of relatives around crowded dining room tables, especially on Sundays and holidays. To have 3 or 4 different conversations going at the same time was perfectly normal. And we would all bounce in and out of several of the ongoing conversations.

I also know people who would be driven crazy by that. They like quiet table conversation, with no more than one conversation happening at any given point.

I say what I mean. That is why I sometimes keep silent.

As a young woman, I had a couple of jobs that let me observe lots of couples interacting. It helped teach me behavior traps that I knew I did not want to fall into in my own life.

For example, picture a bustling, upscale restaurant, with lots of happy people chatting, dining, and enjoying their night out. Sometimes I observed some couple having dinner but not speaking a word to each other. They were not angry. They did not seem upset at all.

They often started out with a drink, followed by appetizers. After salad, came their entrees, and perhaps dessert. They were having a lovely evening, but they spoke more with their waiter than with each other.

When I saw these lengthy dinners in silence, even though jovial conversations filled the air around them, I knew I would *not* want to be in such a relationship.

All I could think was, "How could they possibly have nothing to say to each other?" I was dumbfounded. If I love someone, I can't wait to share with them the delights of each day, or the sorrows or worries that arise, or the dreams and thoughts I am developing.

Decades later the memories from those restaurant observations flashed back to me. It happened on an evening on which my husband and I finished driving 12 hours to get to my parents' home.

We turned in early, leaving the "old folks" to burn the late night oil. Before we drifted off to sleep, I could hear Mom and Dad chatting away about the day's activities and discussing a few news stories they'd seen on TV.

Suddenly, Ron whispered to me, "Who's *out* there?"

"My parents," I replied.

"No, no, no," he insisted. "Who are they talking *to*?"

"Um," I started. "Each other."

"Whyyy?" he sincerely and innocently asked.

"It's… called… conversation," was all I could think to say.

He then literally said, "They still talk to each other?"

We had a great laugh over that particular thinking of Ron's. Those are the sorts of nuances that I lovingly call "Ronnerisms."

Sure, at the time, my parents had already been married to each other for 65 years. They are truly each other's dearest friend. Who better to share our thoughts, fears, concerns, dreams, opinions, and passions with then our best friend?

John Gehrisch emphasizes the importance of the example set by parents on our future personal relationships and how we perceive and treat our partners. His own parents' 50+ happy years together inspired his positive thinking as Gehrisch developed the "Bimbo's" companion book, "The Golf Pro Has Heart."

Tip: If you are married to someone you do not consider to be your best friend, don't work on the marriage. Work on the friendship with your spouse. A great marriage will be one of the gleeful results.

My parents, Robert and Glenna Burnham,
celebrating their 65th Wedding Anniversary, June 24, 2015.
Photo Credit: Jim Bowman

Section 6
FEELINGS

21
No Holds Barred

*Life can be a comedy for those who think <u>and</u> feel,
but a tragedy for those who only think <u>or</u> feel.*

The way we feel can dramatically impact the way we behave. Even people who purport to be purely logical have feelings.

"Hi, how are you?"

"Fine, thank you. And you?" Actually, at any given moment in our day, we are experiencing a wide range of emotions, and to varying degrees.

We simply choose not to totally answer the question with some response such as "Actually, I feel a little nervous. I have a big review at work tomorrow. Generally, I feel confident and alright, but I didn't sleep well, so I am a little more tired than I like. I'm also confused. My girlfriend kept trying to pick a fight with me yesterday, and whatever was going on has yet to be resolved."

That's not what was being asked, though it sounded like, "How are you?" It was just a casual expression of greeting.

Then there are times when we *should* express feelings. Some of us express feelings easily. For others, emotional expression is difficult.

We all know people who wear their hearts on their sleeves, so to speak. We all also know people who internalize their feelings, bottling everything up inside.

Whether we admit it or not, express them openly or not, recognize emotions or not, we all have them.

We experience a wide range of feelings, from feeling wise, wanted, and worthy to unwise, unpopular, or even washed up. We may feel promising, popular, sexy, and attractive. We may feel unwanted, unattractive or timid.

We can be annoyed, uncomfortable and sad. We can be filled with anger and discontent. We feel woeful, vulnerable, confused, or embarrassed. Or we feel gratitude, affection, interest, and peaceful.

Circumstances affect how confident or fragile we feel. Or how positively or negatively we see ourselves.

Regardless, it can be inspiring to recognize all the many nuances within our emotional ranges, as they rise and fall like waves rolling on the ocean.

I've heard that 80% of our conversation uses just 2,000 words. Emotional words take up only a tiny fraction of that. And yet, the range of words that express our emotions is vast. We need not lack the precise words to describe how we feel at any given time.

Consider the following words that will give you more than 400 words and expressions to help you better communicate and reflect on the vast spectrum of feelings we can have.

Loathing, hateful, infuriated, hostile, furious, enraged
Hated, despised, cheated, reviled, loathed, despicable, insufferable
Calloused, cynical, uncompromising, pessimistic
Arrogant, conceited, haughty, egotistical, big-headed
Proud, overconfident
Bad, evil, wicked, corrupt, unscrupulous, ruthless
Mad, angry, ticked off, disgusted, annoyed, bitter, violent, irritated
Fuming, livid, heated, cross, fractious, peevish, touchy, testy
Irritated, agitated, impatient, indignant, vexed, outraged, piqued
Shameful, disgraceful, appalling, inferior, mediocre, substandard,
Humiliated, embarrassed, chagrined, degraded, ashamed, self-conscious
Guilty, remorseful, mortified, awkward
Unprofessional, disloyal, treacherous, fickle, untrustworthy, perfidious
Dishonest, deceitful, unfair, insincere, fraudulent, corrupt
Cold, unfriendly, unsympathetic, stony, icy, unkind, distant

Unhappy, unneeded, depressed, blue, miserable, disheartened, down
Despair, dismal, gloomy, dreary, bleak, dull
Resentful, revengeful, vindictive, implacable, ruthless
Out of control, frantic, panicky, desperate, uptight
Edgy, defensive, wary, quarrelsome
Dissatisfied, disillusioned, disappointed, thwarted
Underappreciated, underpaid, underrated, undereducated, stretched
Overwhelmed, drowning, claustrophobic, suffocating, restricted
Misunderstood, misjudged, misread
Stifled, smothered, stagnant, stunted, passed by, held back, inhibited
Antagonistic, aggressive, belligerent, destructive, bellicose, pugnacious
Ignored, insignificant, unimportant, trivial
Withdrawn, worn out, wrongly accused
Weak, frail, sick, resigned, pained, fragile, puny
Lethargic, indifferent, tired, fatigued, exhausted, down and out, defeated
Empty, devastated, drifting, confounded, drained
Indecisive, irresolute, faltering, dithering
Naïve, dopey, immature, green
Uncertain, unsure, nervous, off balance, jumpy, nervy
Inexperienced, insecure, inferior, inadequate, incapable, ineffective
Hollow, shallow, superficial
Jealous, envious, desirous, invidious
Yearning, pining, wistful
Shy, self-conscious, inhibited, intimidated, bashful, restrained
Confused, perplexed, puzzled, mixed up, foggy, disoriented
Baffled, bewildered
Discombobulated, concerned, worried, troubled, apprehensive
Burned out, worn out, tired, regretful,
Moody, temperamental, morose, short-tempered, grumpy
Brooding, ominous, menacing, gloomy, ruminating, contemplative
Challenged, tested, confrontational
Weepy, upset, torn up, sad, sullen, futile, forlorn
Unloved, trapped, reviled, despised
Used, unheard, hurt
Abused, battered, bruised, belittled, broken, demeaned, put down
Unfaithful, untrue, adulterous, faithless, traitorous
Undisciplined, wild, unruly, disobedient, willful
Dependent, needy, reliant
Out of shape, overweight
Obnoxious, unbearable, insufferable
Reluctant, unwilling, disinclined, hesitant
Suspicious, disbelieving, cautious, apprehensive, anxious,
Betrayed, let down

Dismayed, discontented, dejected, crestfallen, disgruntled, dissatisfied
Worthless, useless, rejected, neglected, failure, hopeless, helpless
Pushed, provoked, incited, aggravated
Lustful, hot, immodest, licentious
Lonely, left out, left behind, isolated, excluded, estranged
Abandoned, alienated, alone
Undecided, unsure, tentative,
Uncomfortable, threatened, tense, resistant,
Terrified, afraid, frightened, worried, scared, panicky, hysterical
Pressured, overcommitted, hectic, frustrated, exasperated, exhausted
Fed up, dejected, despondent, unfulfilled
Apathetic, ambivalent, indifferent, listless, lethargic
Bored, uninterested, jaded
Awkward, difficult
Apologetic, sorry, rueful
Empathetic, compassionate
Sympathetic, concerned, understanding
Numb, unfeeling, dazed, distressed, disoriented
Warm, tender, relaxed, unperturbed
Affectionate, demonstrative, kind, caring
Consoled, cared for
Pitied, pitiful, pathetic
Patient, calm, comfortable, content
Sensitive, thoughtful
Curious, inquisitive, nosy, probing
Tempted, lured
Restless, fidgety
Confused, scatter-brained, lost, foolish
Streetwise, smart, superior, worldly, sophisticated, mature
Surprised, shocked, stunned, awed, amazed
Idolized, revered
Infatuated, interested, interesting, fascinating, remarkable
Hopeful, buoyant, eager
Determined, gritty, resolute, unwavering, strong-minded
Committed, devoted, steadfast, loyal, trusted
Energetic, energized, hyper, peppy, animated, spirited, robust, lively
Excited, enthusiastic, thrilled, whole-hearted
Good, respectable, virtuous
Friendly, welcoming, approachable, outgoing, sociable
Fun, amusing, cool
Graceful, elegant, smooth
Sexy, sensual, racy
Attractive, appealing, adored

Loved, liked, love struck
Stable, sure, secure
Pleased, happy, elated, amused
Peaceful, equanimous, even-tempered, at ease, blissful
Enchanted, delighted, bewitched
Joyful, jolly, joking, cheerful, jovial
Intelligent, smart, brilliant
Creative, inspired, imaginative, inventive
Included, important, influential, affirmed
Destined, fated, preordained
Kind, caring, gentle
Benevolent, munificent
Safe, protected
Vibrant, turned on, passionate, focused, alive, alert, energetic
Daring, competitive, courageous, brave, protective
Giving, generous
Strong, capable, independent
Effective, efficient, disciplined
Zealous, driven, valiant
Venturesome, unlimited, anticipating
Ready, respected, responsible, professional, on track, optimistic
Satisfied, relieved, proud, fulfilled
Happy, great, glad
Honored, gratified, satisfied, esteemed, approved, admired
Forgiving, merciful, tolerant
Successful, significant, prosperous
Honest, true, candid, faithful
Free, able, unrestricted

Whether we are expressing verbally or non-verbally, we <u>are</u> feeling and exuding emotions. Don't hold back. We are colorful beasts. Both positive and negative feelings are valid. I always felt this is one big reason that a roller coaster is more exciting than a merry-go-round… and why gloomy or stormy weather helps us appreciate fair or sensational weather.

Tip: For the most fulfilling life, always strive to truly *feel yourself living*.

22
Empathy

A couple with whom we socialize has a couple of lovely large dogs. Unfortunately, time starts catching up… aging dogs develop challenges.

Barkkie seemed on his last legs… literally. His spirits remained stable, but his body just wasn't what it used to be. His humans struggled with the pending loss of their beloved Barkkie… how much time did they have left with him? And, more importantly, was he suffering? *That* they did *not* want.

With my husband, I shared the challenge our friends were suffering with Barkkie. He loves these folks, so his response caught me off balance. "Well, they don't need two large dogs anyway."

What???!!!?? THAT was not the issue… what about the pain and heartbreak they feel? My jaw had dropped. I tried to make him understand… They are empty-nesters, my love. These dogs are like children to them. They love them. They are family. My husband repeated his cold comment. Hmmm…

"Darling, do you mean if one of your children was suffering and passed, your friends should simply note that you have four, so losing one should not be a problem?"

Now I had his attention.

He feels physical empathy to the point where he "gets" physical symptoms, if a friend describes something they are or have suffered. However, his logic challenged him to feel emotional empathy for our friends' struggle with their precious Barkkie. "It's only a dog. It's not a human."

Well, there it is. You either have empathy or you don't, I guess. My hubby has many strengths, but emotional empathy is not one of them. Duh.

He loves these friends. He loves dogs. I know he actually felt bad that they were hurting in their loss. However, *expressing* empathy is not one of his great capabilities.

We all "get" the logic of aging and the preference to avoid suffering. We don't all deal well with the emotion and pain of loss. In fact, most of us simply break down now and then. Recovery is difficult, and it's something we all handle differently.

Empathy, in my opinion, **should** come first. When someone we care about struggles with a personal challenge, it is a blessing to be able to put ourselves in their shoes and feel for them. That is how we are able to share strength and support for those we love. We are stronger when we know we are not alone. When we empathize, we offer support, compassion, love.

If we can't, we stand alone. We don't get it. Life is better when we "get" it. We need to dare to show we care. That means being vulnerable.

"Home on the Range of Emotions"

Anticipation
>He'll be home soon and I want everything perfect.
>>I've worked hard, and everything looks right.

Enthusiasm
>Take a fresh shower and do my hair.
>>Dress up pretty (change three times).

Disappointment
>He's forgotten; no response to my text.
>>A couple more hours pass by.

Acceptance
>Struggle to keep sadness from turning bitter.
>>Just keep busy, busy… work some more.

Renewal
>He arrives home, and I gleefully bound to greet him.
>>Nada. Bupkiss. Nothing… not even a slight hello.

Rejection
     Crabby. Nasty. Critical. Grumpy. And mean.
        As usual, he saved all that just for me alone.

Questioning
     Why do I keep setting myself up for this?
        Hope lives eternal in the heart of a dog.

When we read, hear, or learn something very emotional or personal or difficult, it is natural to relate emotionally. We empathize with the feelings we perceive in the scenario.

Tear down the walls that protect our vulnerabilities. Those walls hold us back.

Tip: Don't hold back. Dare to try and put yourself in someone else's situation to better understand… to feel… to empathize.

23
Dousing the Anger Flame

*Some days he just doesn't have
enough middle fingers to go around.*

"I'm sorry, but you make me soooo mad!"

Actually, I can only *inspire* positive or negative feelings. I can't actually "make" someone else angry any more than I can "make" them happy.

These are personal, internal decisions over which we each have full control. If I am blaming someone else for my anger or crediting someone else with my happiness, I am passing the buck. I am faking myself out. I am trying to deny that I have full responsibility for my reactions.

Think of times when someone has tried to offer an apology, but they turned it around and actually blamed their bad behavior on you. No true apology comes with a caveat that, "I'm sorry I did such-and-such or said whatever, but it was *your* fault. *You* made me do that."

That's an attempted deflection of personal responsibility, at best… and a false accusation in any case.

Flashpoint
Money often lights the spark in stress-related anger. One or the other spouse did not realize that there wasn't enough money in the checking account or else they forgot to send a check or whatever. Suddenly, there it is… an overdue payment notice.

When anger is triggered, success is ours if we let cooler heads prevail.

Most importantly, everyone wins if we calmly sit down and work out a plan to help avoid such unpleasant surprises in the future.

In some households, this means writing out a budget, listing every dollar going both in and out… and sticking to it. Budgets should also be revisited and adjusted every few months.

In other cases, we can solve late payment issues by setting up automatic payments, though it's important to keep a list of such payments so that we don't think we have more funds available in our bank account than we actually will once automatic payments are drawn out.

In still other cases, it may just be a matter of sitting down together to write the checks needed that month and then putting them in their stamped and addressed envelopes and marking a date on each one to know when each should be placed in the mail, allowing plenty of time for payments to both arrive and be processed.

Whatever systems work, and whatever the issues may be, work together on the solutions, rather than ranting about the problems. Your lover is not the enemy, no matter how much you may sometimes wish you could simply dump all the blame on them.

Turn Down the Heat

I like to think of ways to reduce frustrations. Sometimes the fixes are so simple, we don't even see them.

For instance, many couples squabble about the toothpaste tube. One squeezes it in the middle, and the other prefers to neatly roll it up from the end. The resulting angst renews daily, every time either one brushes their teeth. Ummm… why not just buy two tubes of toothpaste, so each has their own?

It matters little what has inspired our annoyance or anger. Emotions tend to flair. We can take a time out. At least we must remain open to our partner calling for a time out.

Go for a run. Read a book. Explain that you are leaving the room (or the house), and when you return you will try to talk again. Give it 30 minutes.

However, we should not say something counterproductive like "when *you've* had a chance to think about it." *That* only sounds blaming and sarcastic.

During a squabble or a time out, it's important to not merely "disappear," or rush off to a bar, or do anything else that could add a layer of frustration and disappointment to the ongoing scenario. This needs to be a peaceful, non-judgmental time.

This is very difficult for some people to do. Inability to contain or suppress our own anger, often means we have no interest in toning it down, never mind considering that we may actually be part of the problem.

Violence and aggression are not just a part of man's nature. Plenty of women are equally violent and aggressive. Psychologists note that whether or not such tendencies are *in* someone's nature typically matters far less than the ways in which we were nurtured, particularly early in our lives.

Children may be told "no" when they act out, but if there are no consequences, they start to feel entitled to lash out whenever it suits them. An out-of-control child typically grows into an out-of-control teenager and adult.

They never were taught skills to respond productively or positively when handling challenges or opposition. Lashing out, verbally, physically and psychologically has worked since they can remember.

Some situations that will trigger explosions from them can be highly predictable, but others seem to come out of nowhere and for no obvious reason. Blow-ups can be large or small, predictable or sudden.

Blow Ups

Guests were coming for dinner the following night. Raelene and Steven had planned and discussed the menu… steak, baked potatoes, salad, and asparagus. Then she asked which item that they had pre-prepared might be Steven's preference for a Happy Hour snack… chips with onion dip or the marinated baby mozzarella cheese balls with roasted peppers and some crackers.

Out of the blue, he blew!

"Neither!" He continued in a rant, "You always do this. There's too much food. For 10 years I've begged you not to do this. Still you *always* do it!"

"Hmmm," Raelene thought. "I always do what? Is it the conversation to plan the meal we'll present? Is it involving him, rather than just putting out snacks once the guests arrive?"

Raelene knew full well that as he poured glasses of wine, he'd ask what she was serving as an appetizer. Her mistake seemed to be inviting his input ahead of time.

Meanwhile, Steven wondered why she'd then explained to him that she was feeling off balance, nervous to talk with him. This conversation had been a typical example of something that she saw as a benign, non-threatening, casual conversation. Yet, it was something that triggered an out-of-proportion negative reaction from him.

This wasn't always the norm. However, it occurred often enough to form a negative pattern.

So, she continued to exist with the feeling that she was walking on eggshells, never sure which step would crack one and "release the Kraken," uh, er, I mean, his wrath.

Later, in a calm time, Raelene tried to mention it, asking Steven if perhaps he'd been in pain or over-tired or trying to focus on something else.

He just ranted again that she'd better stop it. "*You* are out of control!"

It's easy to see who really was out of control, though none of us could know just *why* Steven was wound so tight.

You don't have to be a therapist or psychologist to recognize that something else is going on here. Perhaps he was jealous because she would be getting compliments as a good cook. Perhaps he wasn't interested in talking about the dinner plans. Perhaps he felt insecure and thus needed to push her "down" in an ill-attempt to feel better about himself.

Perhaps he is a "Control Freak" and didn't like her seeming in charge of something, even something as simple as the appetizers. Perhaps he felt left out, or maybe he had wanted to make or help make the food, but he lacked the maturity or confidence to express himself or share a need that he felt.

What We Can Do

It's far more pleasant to be able to deal with someone calmly. But if a husband suggests to his wife that he wants to work on their communication so they can get to a better place together, her response is important. We saw this with Mark and Sharon in Chapter 17, "Man versus Woman."

If she says that she would like that also, they are in a good starting place. If she sarcastically snarls that he doesn't know how to communicate, they've got a long way to go.

If your partner expresses anger or instant rage over things that don't seem provocative, there's a problem. Duh. And *you* will typically feel the finger of blame pointing at you. There's nothing you do to cause or prevent it, despite insistent protests that it's all your fault.

I've been there. I get it. Out of seemingly nowhere the angry tone prevailed, bellowing down on *me*, the person he said he loves. This can happen to anyone, even people who are typically very loving.

For example, Chip and Zoe were boating one weekend. She had served breakfast dockside for some friends. Now they were on the boat at the dock and preparing to hang out. At Chip's request, she turned on her laptop to help him re-establish the boat's internet connection. Once successful, she then turned her attention to straightening up the cabin to get everything secured and ship shape.

"I can't stand it," Chip snarled out of the blue. "You are always working on that damn computer. I'm throwing it away!" (Reality check: Zoe hadn't even turned it on for three days.)

As with me, Zoe's past had taught her not to go toe-to-toe with *anyone* ranting. Still, as she walked away, she muttered to herself, "*You* should throw your creepy attitude away."

Five minutes passed. She was straightening up the small galley (boat kitchen) where he'd had some of his things spread out. He'd now moved them, and she was putting away their new groceries.

"What the F*@! are you doing now?" His ranting continued. "I need you above. What are you doing?!?"

"Just putting the food away, *Sweetness*," Zoe replied, only semi-masking her sarcasm. "When you need my help you just need to ask, not yell."

"Bullshit," came his immediate and angry retort. "You do exactly what you want, when you want. I can't stand it."

Thanks to the wisdom of age and experience, Zoe chose to ignore his senseless anger and attack. There was no point to call attention to the lack of logic. She certainly knew there was no gain to bring up the fact that his attacks were very hurtful. He was, obviously, having a bad day.

Oops! My Bad

Chip fired up the boat's engines. Then, without a word, he started pulling the boat out of the slip.

"We're still tied back here," Zoe immediately called out as she scurried up on deck and swiftly moved to unhook the aft lines from the cleats.

"WHAT?!??" came his startled but ferocious voice. "You said you untied them." (Umm… Zoe had said nothing at all.)

Every time they prepare to leave the dock, they go through a routine. He likes to handle engine preps, forward lines, and power cables to be sure nothing is forgotten. She waits on the back on the swim platform for his "word" from the captain's chair. Then she unties those two final lines and gives him the "all clear" to go ahead.

On "anger," even her dearest Chip's brain did not function clearly, not even for a time-tested and long-practiced routine. I wasn't even on deck. Yet, because he'd nearly goofed up badly, he needed to yell at someone, and I was the one nearby. Bad choice, but we're all human.

I get it. I have a boating hubby, too. Out on the water, other boaters tend to annoy my Captain Ron with their mariner's skills… or, I should say, their *lack* of mariner's skills. "Some people just shouldn't be allowed to boat. They don't know what they're doing!" He has a most gruff snarl.

"Here, dear, have a Snickers Bar." No, I don't always say it out loud, but the humorous 2015-16 TV commercials surely come to mind. "You're just not yourself when you're hungry." Sigh.

Irritatingly angry people have no sense of humor when wearing their "angry pants."

So, I've learned to not take things personally. *We* do not cause *their* anger. We can, however, exacerbate it… or we can defuse it.

Sometimes I'm just glad when grumpy behavior comes out in succession all in one day. For me, it's better to endure someone having one bad day than someone who always has grumpy days.

Sadness Lives Inside

Sometimes people house a great deal of anger and resentment and distrust inside, and it manifests itself in negative talk and behavior, even many, many years later. If someone feels they were wronged in life, they need to get to a better place, personally, to have healthy relationships.

Other-wise, they will inevitably take out their ill feelings on their unwitting spouse, who is *not* responsible for their trauma nor its present day manifestations.

Many people have grown up in families with a raging alcoholic or other drug addict, and they've tolerated a wide array of poor behaviors and treatment as a result.

Some were raised in homes with tremendous anger and yelling and disrespect. Far too many saw their childhoods literally slammed with physical, emotional, and psychological abuse.

Even if we try to be strong and recognize that these behaviors were not right, it's amazing how often we repeat them ourselves when we become adults. In fact, psychologists often tell us that people who feel that they were treated poorly as children or in early adult relationships, tend to become angry, belligerent, and even aggressive adults, taking their angst out on loved ones.

I was blessedly raised in a healthy family without yelling, alcohol or other abuses. I think I was 17 before I heard my father say, "Darn."

That's not to say that everything was "peaches and cream." I can remember parental rules cast upon us that we felt were unfair and without reason, other than being a way to get us out of our parents' hair, so to speak. My older sister and I agreed that if we ever had children of our own, we would *never* say such things.

Lo and behold, years went by. I was at my sister's house and overheard her scolding her daughter, using some of the exact phrases we'd scowled at our mother for using when we were children… the very same words we'd vowed to never say if we had children.

When Deborah and I spoke alone later, I told her what I'd overheard her say to her daughter. I reminded her that we'd promised we'd never say those things to any child of our own.

"Oh, my!" She gasped, "You're right. I'd forgotten."

Now, you should understand that my sister is a truly gentle, healing soul. I've often said that she is the closest thing to a living angel that I know on this earth. She would never knowingly say an unkind word to anyone. But we are *all* human.

Mere Mortals

Making a mistake is human. We become better people when we don't follow a mistake with choices that make the mistake even worse. Thus, it's important not to try to justify our poor choices. What we need to do, is learn to do better so that we don't repeat bad behavior.

It's more challenging if you are someone who has found a peaceful and positive way of dealing with life, and yet, you are in a relationship with someone who is highly unsettled.

We hear of too many situations which end in deadly violence between two people who loved each other. One of them was using anger, aggression, and violence instead of calmness, love, or logic. No one wins. Everyone loses.

It's not easy to help a belligerent person find their way without enabling their violent anger. Yet, when we love someone, we may well need to do exactly that.

Anger Management… the Victim's Perspective

Though it is difficult, at best, do not try to reason with an angry person if they have been drinking. Though you may want to tell them straight out that they cannot keep treating you the way they are, do not say things that are apt to incite more anger.

It's not easy to survive these storms without also coming across as a weak, snivelling victim.

You can't "win" an argument with an angry person. You can agree with them, including agreeing to discuss the problem at a specific, but later time… when they are sober, calm, etc.

However, you might want to choose to say "we" when referring to negative things.

For example, "when *we* are sober" or "when *we* are calm" or even "when *I* am sober," even if you already are. The idea is to diffuse a volatile situation, while validating the angry person's needs. Their lack of logic is irrelevant.

Sometimes it seems that nothing will work, but other times, we can be quite effective if we try any of the following.

- If you can get them thinking about something else, something that is not upsetting, that can help.

- Agree with them that they have been wronged, even if you have not wronged them.

- Always keep your voice volume low. If they speak louder, speak even softer.

- Never go toe-to-toe with them in a verbal battle, unless you really want to see it escalate out of control.

- Do let them know that their feelings are legitimate; say nothing to diminish their "right" to feel the way they do.

Just remember, you are likely not a professional therapist or a psychologist. Do not put yourself in danger. Don't get so caught up in trying to help someone who is out of control that you risk your own safety.

No conversations with an angry person can be positive as long as they are "bouncing off the walls." De-escalate the situation. Stay safe.

Tip: If enraged, don't engage.

24
Trust, But Verify

"Cheat on a marriage by having an affair
with your spouse."
-- Dr. Mark Goulston (1948 -)
American author and advisor

In our closest relationships, I believe we should be able to take trust for granted. With so many undisciplined, untrustworthy human beings in our midst, however, trust gets readily bruised and broken, sometimes repeatedly. We then find ourselves in the unhappy reality of the oxymoron, "trust, but verify."

During the Cold War between the USA and the USSR, "trust, but verify" became part of President Ronald Reagan's 1980's standard lingo. He repeated this whenever he spoke of how relations were going between the two Super Powers, especially with reference to Mikhail Gorbachev.

The old, Russian proverb speaks of the *desire* to trust, but also recognizes the *need* to verify. Reagan used "trust, but verify" with regard to Soviet military weapons, specifically missiles.

He wanted the USA to be able to trust that the Soviets were indeed dismantling, as they claimed. However, a history of lies meant that he needed proof that they were actually destroying the number of missiles they claimed to be reducing.

When applied to our love relationships, unfortunately, trust is sometimes not enough either. We want to be able to trust, but time and experience with a particular individual may have taught us otherwise.

Trust may have been broken… badly. Verification becomes vital for both sanity and survival.

"The truly scary thing about undiscovered lies is that they have a greater capacity to diminish us than exposed ones. They erode our strength, our self-esteem, our very foundation."

-- Cheryl Hughes (1967 -)
American author

Worn out phrases, such as "What she doesn't know won't hurt her" are total bologna. Anyone who has been on the receiving end of their partner lying or cheating knows they and their relationship were hurting before they learned of the illicit deceit. They just didn't specifically know "why" or "what was going on" with their spouse. Verification is not needed unless trust has been broken between the two people in the relationship. Crumbling trust does not happen on its own. Nor does it happen quickly.

That said, trust, once broken, does not merely heal on its own as time passes by. Time is needed, most assuredly... usually a very long time, in fact. But to heal, the wounded party needs both time and truth. Truth is typically very difficult for a liar and cheater, but it is necessary to rebuild shattered trust.

Without trust, our relationships lack an essential ingredient for emotional intimacy. We need to be able to totally trust our partner with our deepest thoughts, dreams, fears, and secrets.

This trust means that they will never throw our pain and vulnerabilities in our face. Trust means we know they will protect us and our innermost thoughts and shared feelings without question.

When we have true emotional intimacy, all other types of intimacy become easy and natural. We can trust without any need for verification.

Tip: Trust delivers a much healthier and happier love life.

Section 7
SEX, SEX, SEX

25
The Intimacy High Five

"I'm certain that most couples expect to find intimacy in marriage, but it somehow eludes them."

-- James Dobson (1936 -)
American psychologist

Intimacy is way more than sex, although most of us think first of sexual intimacy when we hear the word "intimacy."

Intimacy is not something instantaneous in a relationship. It develops over time. Some intimacies are sparked quickly. Others evolve much more slowly.

Intimacy is something we share verbally and nonverbally. To have true intimacy, we must also have full trust and feel safe with our partner. Intimacy reflects varying levels of closeness and special sharing. Bonding moments make relationships stronger and more fulfilling.

Completing the Intimacy High Five means wholeness in a relationship between two people. The five levels of intimacy to which I refer include sexual, physical, intellectual, emotional, and spiritual.

Sexual Intimacy

Sexual intimacy comes into play at some point in the growing relationship. It starts with flirting. Our facial expressions, from "that certain smile" to a "knowing wink," all share our sexual desires.

This is why anyone in love with a person who continues to flirt with others outside the relationship knows a great deal of pain. Their lover is literally sharing a special sexual intimacy with someone else. We humans can be so insensitive sometimes.

We forget how uplifting it felt to have a "person of special interest" flirt with us. We think it means that they want us. How very disheartening to find they simply want everyone. Yikes. It's downright creepy when we look at it that way.

Flirting leads to special, leading conversations. Ultimately, we get to sex itself. Sex is sex, regardless of which specific acts we choose. Intercourse is not the only act of sex, by any means. (This is true, regardless of whether or not a particular sex act is acknowledged as "sex" by former President Bill Clinton or not.)

Sex should be happy and fun, warm and loving, joyous and giving. With time, repetition, and a lot of trust, sexual intimacy remains a most precious facet of a healthy, loving relationship.

Still, even with extreme frequency, it should be welcomed as a gift, not expected as if it is some daily commandment. No one wants to feel like their sexual activity is merely something their partner looks at in the same way as brushing their teeth or combing their hair.

Physical Intimacy

Physical intimacy is one of the first types of intimacy experienced by a couple. Activities together reflect physical intimacy. For example, recreational activities such as walking, hiking, boating, dancing, swimming, listening to music at a concert, and playing tennis together are all physical intimacy activities when done with a "person of special interest."

The same goes for shared activities such as cooking, dining, going to happy hour, visiting a museum, or even shopping. There's no physical intimacy unless activities are done with a "person of special interest." He goes fishing while she goes shopping reflects a lack of physical intimacy.

Physical intimacy is not the same as sexual intimacy, though sex is definitely physical. Here, however, we are referring to all the physical intimacy activities that are not associated with sex.

This can be as basic as getting into someone's "space," by brushing against them, touching an arm while talking, or letting knees or feet touch under a table.

It also includes personal touching that reflects fondness or love, such as holding hands, hugging, or kissing. These are flirtatious touches, but *without* a *direct* goal of sex.

This helps us understand why we are tinkering with risk if we engage in activities with an individual other than our partner. Most affairs begin at work or in regular activities with someone other than our spouse. That's logical. Humans lack self-discipline and we are quick to rationalize bad choices in behavior.

"Well, my wife doesn't like to go running."

"But my husband is always too busy."

What begins in relative innocence easily progresses to other intimacies. This is most often based on opportunity.

Intellectual Intimacy

The slippery slope of inappropriately shared intimacy starts in other areas as well. Let's look at intellectual intimacy. Early in our relationships we talk easily and excitedly about a wide variety of topics. No subject seems off base.

We truly want to get to know what this person thinks about issues of the day, their family, their activities, and their interests. We hungrily seek the details surrounding their dreams and goals.

Earnest conversation evolves into discussions of work and career, values and fears, beliefs and concerns. Soon these honest conversations lead to true friendship, caring, respect, and a heaping serving of self-acceptance.

This does not mean that you may think alike on all issues. For example, my husband and I typically vote differently, although many of our political ideals seem parallel.

When it comes to sports, the pattern continues. In baseball, he's an avid New York Yankees fan, while I have followed the Boston Red Sox all my life. It's one of the greatest sports rivalries of all time, and we are never on the same side.

Whether you and your mate agree is not what's most vital. What *is* paramount is that there is mutual respect for differing ideas, thoughts, and opinions… and that we never stop sharing them.

Challenges arise if we start thinking we know everything about our own partner, and we stop talking about true topics of interest.

Gabbing starts getting limited to daily lists of what needs to be done. We no longer express interest in that wonderful, intriguing person inside. We don't take the time. We don't give the time.

However, we often go astray if we *do* open up to someone *other* than our own beloved. A new person hasn't yet heard all our stories fifty times. Their interests appear refreshing and curiosity-sparking. Their reciprocal interest in every little thing we say or every joke we tell is very appealing.

We goof up big time if we are willing to give someone else our intellectual interest and energy at the sacrifice of our own spouse. This is a sad story that is repeated far too often. In truth, if we gave our spouse even half the time and interest and conversation we give to this new person, we'd likely be quickly reminded of just why we fell in love with them in the first place.

Emotional Intimacy

With time, intellectual intimacy slides into emotional intimacy. We find ourselves not just interested in *what* a person has to say, but we also start to *care*. We notice how they feel when they talk about a rotten marriage or overbearing boss. We want to help end the personal injustices that are hurting them. We care that someone is not treating them well.

We are not just sharing stories about issues and interests. We've moved to sharing feelings and inner thoughts.

We now hunger to know their dreams and goals. We are fascinated by the passions that make them tick. We start to feel a highly bonding connection… a connection that would hurt to lose.

When we are getting to know someone, we certainly don't build intellectual or emotional intimacy in front of television shows or while playing video games. We do this one on one. We do this with open and frequent meaningful conversations. We do this with active listening. We do this with quality time together.

Emotional intimacy elevates our caring to new levels. It deepens our love, respect, and compassion. It thrives on complete and total trust.

Spiritual Intimacy

One of the most challenging and yet fulfilling types of intimacy is spiritual intimacy. Too often, couples don't even discuss their spirituality. They'll talk about every subject going… except religion or faith.

Sometimes the subject of faith gets discussed when plans are being made to get married. It should have hit center stage long before that.

Reality remains contrary.

However, as relationships evolve, the need for spiritual completeness usually surfaces. This development could follow some trauma, a personal health challenge, a loss in the family, or other dramatic event. Whatever inspires it, this urge should be followed.

When we share faith, we become stronger. We can pray together. We accept that our faith gives us extra strength.

We know that we don't have to possess all the answers. We get stronger by placing our faith in a power that is far greater than even our strongest love.

It's a beautiful thing when a couple can share and practice faith together. We are bolstered by the support system of the faith and congregation we find that most closely reflects our beliefs. We enjoy the secrets, strength, and solidarity of spiritual intimacy with God.

The closest, most loving relationships enjoy all five intimacies… sexual, physical, intellectual, emotional, and spiritual. Most of us feel pretty good if we enjoy any of the intimacies with our partner. Reaching true intimacy in all five areas is a worthy goal to enjoy a healthy, loving relationship.

If you are part of a fortunate couple that has already achieved all five intimacies, congratulations! On every day that you know you and your beloved share all five, give each other that Intimacy High Five! You've earned it. You deserve to share that knowing celebration with each other.

Tip: Genuine intimacy is the foundation of the most beautiful love relationships.

26
<u>Let's Get Intimate, Intimate</u>

Only newlyweds and liars have sex every day.

When Olivia Newton John sang the hit song, "Let's Get Physical," plenty of fun rang out with double meanings… intentional or intimated. Did the lyrics suggest getting physically fit or "getting it on" in a sexual way? It matters little. Interpretation is open to every individual.

In relationships, intimacy is vital… or we really don't have a relationship. As we've said, intimacy reigns in many areas, though the first thing that pops into most minds is sex… the physical / sexual intimacy of two people entwined in sexual passion.

Some people focus on the emotional / intellectual intimacy of two people who share thoughts, foibles, passions, dreams, fears, and purpose openly with each other.

That's fine. Intimacy means different things to different people.

Some men consider themselves lucky in life
if the cognac they drink is
older than the woman with whom he sleeps.

When it comes to intimacy with our partner, whether physical or intellectual, cutting corners is never good, especially in the long run.

"She no longer enjoys sex," complained Ken.

"Ah-hem… HE no longer shows he loves me," replied Caroline. "I feel totally used."

We've talked about this earlier. If one partner gradually begins "expecting" sex, it can become just a mundane activity, rather than a playful, intimate expression of love.

If one partner no longer feels loved or valued, then the "expected sexual activity" will cause them to feel used.

So much conversation happens early in a relationship that we can mistakenly start to think that we know everything about each other that we need to know. So, why talk?

Helloooo! He still wants sex, right? Even though they had lots of sex earlier in their relationship, <u>he</u> still wants sex with her.

Well, <u>she</u> still wants communication with him. Even though they talked about absolutely everything earlier in their relationship, she still wants conversation with him.

> *"If you kiss her mind, her body will follow."*
> – Pharrell Williams (1973 -)
> American singer and record producer

If you've had a fight or an argument, communication will get you the best "make-up" sex ever. You could just smile or pull her close in a hug, and enjoy "make-up" sex. However, try making up with heartfelt words and tones *first*. The sex will be even better!

It's that basic. Sure, it's tougher, but it's also more sincere and long lasting and far less shallow.

> *Sex is inherited.*
> *If your parents didn't have sex, there is hardly any chance that you would even be here to have that possibility.*

It's very important to be affectionate because you love someone, *not* just when you want to have sex. Give time, affection, and attention.

There is an undeniable Catch 22 loop here. One person may be trying to get their physical and sexual needs met without meeting their mate's intellectual and emotional needs.

Meanwhile, that partner may be trying to get their intellectual and emotional needs met without meeting their mate's physical and sexual needs.

Both feel short-changed, not desired, and unappreciated.

Often, one gives in and meets the other's needs, selflessly, but the other fails to reciprocate… or they wrongly assume that their lover had the same needs and thus they were met. The resulting Catch 22 usually results in a relationship crash and burn.

We may get by for the short term, but inevitably the one-sidedness of the giving leads to a frustration overload.

We may repeatedly try to get our need for sex or our need for communication met by our partner. If our attempts are met with rejection over and over again, we may eventually stop asking. We tend to give up rather than keep setting ourselves up for regular rejection.

Rejection is painful, be it physical or psychological. It undermines our sense of self, passion, and confidence.

Time for Change

Ken was not ready to believe that he needed to change anything. He did not wish to talk with Caroline, and she was tired of feeling sexually used, with *her* intimacy needs going unmet.

"In truth, Caroline just doesn't *get* me any longer," Ken admitted. "Heck, the new girl at work is a better listener. She really *gets* me. She loves listening to me and really cares about the same things I care about. My wife and I just aren't that close any longer."

What Ken didn't want to hear is the fact that this means he's spending personal time socializing and sharing himself intimately with someone other than his wife. Those conversations may indeed feel more alluring with a new person, but Ken is on a very slippery slope.

Intellectual intimacy leads to emotional intimacy and leads to sexual intimacy.

I'll say it again. If he gave his wife even half as much of that attention, he would likely have such a loving feeling for her that he would hardly notice the other woman at work… or at the bar… or wherever.

I cannot count the times that my husband and I have been out at some restaurant or pub and overheard a man or woman "pouring it on" for some new "prospect." It is remarkable how absolutely every single thing one of them brings up as something *they* enjoy is also, precisely, a favorite thing of the *new* person of interest. They sound sincerely amazed how much they have in common. They absolutely "hang" on each other's every word. Hopefully, they are being honest, because they *are* getting intimate.

Turn Your Lover ON

In general, we look at intimacy in terms of sexuality, since that is what comes to mind most readily. So, what *is* it that really turns people on sexually?

Remember that there are always exceptions, but here's a strong slice of reality. Our masculine side gets most easily turned on both physically and visually. Our feminine side gets most easily turned on intellectually and emotionally.

Right now you are either saying, "Yes, I understand that." Or you are saying, "What?!? No way!"

A physical "turn on" can be as simple as brushing past someone, touching an arm, or rubbing a leg. It can be as direct as sexual manipulation.

A visual "turn on" could come from someone offering up a wink or sexy "come on" facial expression. It could come from seeing someone very attractive enter a room, or it could be as overt as porn, whether online, in a magazine, or in a movie.

An intellectual "turn on" could stem from conversation in which the parties appear genuinely interested in each other's thoughts, opinions, and comments. It can also come from observation of someone giving a presentation or speech, listening to a teacher or professor, or reading someone's written words.

An emotional "turn on" often spills from words that give a partner a sense of sureness and closeness in a relationship, or a touch that is given *without* sex as the "goal." Gestures and words of love, support, concern, and caring can be powerful aphrodisiacs.

Imagine what happens when we fail to recognize the various ways in which different people are inspired. For example, if she satisfies his needs by trying to look attractive to him and by delivering the physical attention he craves, culminating in his regular sexual gratification, he likely feels fulfilled and loved in the relationship.

Let's also say he uses physical groping and fondling to try to turn her on, though she begs for a very different intimacy. Ultimately, she can be left unsatisfied, because she craves feeling his emotional love and sharing the intellectual stimulation expressed through his sincere interest and support of her thoughts, goals, fears, and dreams.

Often he forgets that he actually intellectually and emotionally turned her on early in the relationship. *That* is what first attracted her to him *and* turned her on. She *still* needs that attention… just as *he* still needs the physical and visual attention she showed him early in the relationship.

It matters little which party has gotten lazy about delivering what their partner craves. It doesn't take too many days or weeks for an unsatisfied partner to start to feel love-starved and sadly unfulfilled.

Tip: If you want great sex in the bedroom, show love to each other *outside* the bedroom.

27
<u>Sexual Addiction...Really</u>

How do you know when an addict is lying?
Their lips are moving.

In the 1980's we started to see "sexual addiction" get a great deal of play on television, long before the likes of golf legend Tiger Woods revealed his issues. Doctors lined up to espouse the trauma for these people who simply have to have sex several times a day and with absolutely anybody or everybody, with no regard for anyone else in life.

Hogwash. These are not oversexed people who need more sex than their partners. These are addicts, plain and simple, regardless of their current behavior or drug of choice.

Once someone has been identified with an addiction issue, often with alcohol or some other drug, they are indeed an addict... forevermore. The addictive behaviors may shift in various directions and to different behaviors and substances. Sex is simply a particular addicts' drug of choice.

Recovering alcoholics, who have been sober for a decade or more, still openly classify themselves as alcoholics. They are dealing positively with their addiction every day.

On the other hand, people who say that they "used" to be an addict... hooked on drugs, alcohol, or anything else, are usually missing a very important point. Once someone is an addict, they are always an addict, recovering or otherwise. Thus, a great many addicts kick the habit with one substance only to replace it with another.

Truly vital in helping recovering addicts is building self-discipline. Inner strength. A positive support system. Often addicts lack self-esteem, confidence, and a worthy perception of themselves and their lives.

On the surface, this seems unlikely in otherwise highly successful people, such as superb athletes, movie stars, or professional musicians. They can actually get addicted to their own stardom… their fame… the roar of the crowd, the adulation of their fans. When that wanes, some fall apart.

Any addictive behaviors hurt the addict *and* everyone else around them. Addicts are typically the last ones to see this.

Addicts may have started by having a few too many beers or snorts of cocaine or a quick heroin fix. They were seen by friends as big party animals. The habits got out of control and started controlling their lives.

That, of course, is ridiculously simplified. Yet, it is not off target. If we get hooked on something, be it nicotine, pornography, fame, alcohol, opioids, eating, speed, prescriptions, sex, or other high-risk behaviors, we allow ourselves to be changed. We give up actual control over our lives to some behavior, some substance. Ironically, addicts often think they are *in* control, and if everyone would just leave them alone, they'd be fine.

I recall my father telling me about the first time he drank beer. He didn't do it again, but not because he was some tea-totaling prude.

As a very young man he recognized that the alcohol reduced his inhibitions and made him feel out of control. He didn't like that out-of-control feeling. Even as adults, most of us lack such self-awareness… or we enjoy feeling less inhibited, regardless of how we got there.

We make excuses for ourselves. "I don't want to quit smoking. I enjoy cigarettes."

"I'm not an alcoholic. I'm a social drinker."

"I don't abuse drugs. I just use them to relax."

"I'm not cheating on my husband. What he doesn't know won't hurt him."

Rationalizing. Denying. Making excuses. It's all part of human nature. It's just not one of the better parts.

I don't think we should view sexual addiction any differently. It's sad, like every other addiction. When a person lacks self-discipline, it will manifest itself in a variety of unhappy and unfulfilling ways.

Millions of people in this country are hooked on sugar and don't even know it. Others get so hooked on playing video games that everything else in life gets put on the back burner. The veritable couch potato is actually hooked on watching television... mindlessly... often with little regard for what programs they watch.

Behaviors that we allow to run rampant change us. I've even heard of people who are hooked on running or "working out." They may get physically fit, but little else.

Consider "shopaholics." There's no physical substance being abused, but they can't stop shopping, even once they're thousands of dollars in debt.

Good habits are difficult to create and very easy to break. Unfortunately, bad habits are very easy to create, and they're often extremely difficult to break.

The video game addict. The shopaholic. The Internet fiend. The gambler. The heroin addict. Behaviors that may well have started as entertainment, socializing, distractions, escapes from stress, or even a simple, impulsive urge to try something new, suddenly turn into destructive choices. There may or may not be a physical substance involved.

Regardless, people get hooked. Their behavior alters their brain... triggers hormonal imbalances... changes perspective away from a grasp on a positive reality.

Are they sick? Sure.

Physical addictions are relatively simple to get out of our bodies.
However, a true cure comes with better behavior choices.

Drinkers may stop drinking, but can they learn to establish positive
values, personal goals, and behaviors? If so, they can break the
addictive cycle. If not, they will likely move on to the next
impulsive behavior that will get them hooked on something else, be
it a substance or a behavior.

There's a lot of pain in life, and not just physical. We naturally seek
to escape anxiety, stress and isolation. Many addicts certainly don't
think of themselves as lonely people. Yet, they often are extremely
isolated, or they can feel that way.

This feeling comes from a wide variety of factors. It could be from
trying to cope with a broken family. It could be from trying to lead
a "normal" life in the midst of extreme fame... or extreme domestic
torment. It could be from surviving the horrors and stress of war.
It could be from youthful attempts to "fit in" and feel accepted.

Breaking the patterns of addiction is a science in itself and way
above my pay grade. Unfortunately, most addicts are so deeply
lodged in denial that the primary pain sufferers are their family,
friends, and others who care about them. Again, addicts themselves
tend to feel they'd be fine if everyone would just leave them alone.

Whatever caused the addict's personal self-loathing, isolation,
and/or pain is adrift in the past.

First, we should remember that breaking the physical addiction is
basic and easy. Simple stops there.

Reversing tendencies toward addictive behaviors... breaking the
psychological addiction... is extremely tough and requires forced
compliance or a lifetime commitment to self-discipline.

People around the addict also need support. They can feel as if life has gone crazy. They can believe that everything will be fine if they can only get the addict to see that they are loved and worthy and will be happier when he or she "gets it together."

The addict often scoffs. Everyone *else* is wacky. *They* are just *fine,* remember.

Unfortunately, until an addict "bottoms out," there is usually little we can do to help in the long run. We *can* try to get someone safe. We can try to provide a healthier lifestyle. We can tell them that they are not fooling anyone. We can assure them they are loved. We can encourage them to live better lives.

However, especially with an adult addict, it's out of our hands. We must pray that they don't make choices that end their life or anyone else's. But we cannot make those healthier choices for them.

They must first survive to the point where they acknowledge that they both *need* and *want* help... that they *are* worthy of living a better and happier life.

Tip: This is every bit as true with the sexual addict as it is with the alcoholic or drug addict. Until the adult addict sincerely reaches out for help, God bless them and all those who love them.

28
Sensual versus Sexual

When I get naked in the bathroom,
the shower gets turned on.

Sexy is a decision. We *decide* that our spouse looks sexy to us.
Period. It doesn't matter our age or how long we've been together.

When I make the decision that my husband is the sexiest man I
know, he just plain *is*. Friends scoff, noting his skinny chicken legs
or big beer belly. I scoff right back, noting his contagious laugh,
Paul McCartney puppy dog eyes, brilliant mind, and need for very
frequent sex… with me. I wouldn't have married him if he wasn't
the sexiest man I know.

On the other hand, a person who comes across in a *sexual* way is not
interesting to me. They are exerting power and push. Sexual is
overt, direct, come-and-get-it. Sexual is impersonal, yet overly
friendly. Sexual leaves little to the imagination.

Sleeping Our Way There
In traditional flirtations, women preferred to build emotional
intimacy before moving to sexual intimacy. Men were traditionally
expected to be the ones tending toward multiple sexual partners
with little or no true intimacy beyond sex.

In this day and time, however, many women play by the rules that
were traditionally reserved for men. They increasingly welcome sex
before intimacy. While this may work initially, many people find
this leads to frustration, because eventually they want intimacy,
which is tough to develop after the fact.

We cannot sleep our way to emotional intimacy.

This is why meeting people through the bar scene is usually highly unsatisfying. Bar conversations are not intimate. They are usually lilted with laughter and libations.

However, both men and women express that it's difficult to meet people through other means, especially if they don't want to use technology or a dating program of sorts. I understand. I tried a dating program once. After a couple of lunch dates and beach dates, I found it a little too forced. It wasn't a "natural" way to meet someone, at least not for me.

<u>You</u> are my favorite thing to do!

I always suggest living an active life. Get involved in your community. There are always worthy nonprofit and service organizations through which you will meet lots of new people and be helping great causes at the same time.

You may or may not meet Mr. or Ms. Right, but you will be becoming a better person. It's much healthier than hanging out in bars, too. If you are comfortable going to bars, and you are looking for a dating relationship, try limiting yourself to one or two drinks. Just a suggestion.

My husband and I would never have met if he'd been waiting for it to happen in a bar. That just wasn't my scene. I didn't go into bars, especially not without a man. That's just me.

The Ronald and I met because our offices shared a parking lot, and his window overlooked where we both parked. What I thought were chance conversations over a few weeks with a man who worked near where I worked, turned out *not* to have been just by chance.

No problem. Before he ever asked me out to our first lunch date, our mutual attraction and interest had been well established.

Number Please

Some people think it proves they are sexy when they can get the attentions of *un*available" people, due to physical distance, marital status, career restrictions, etc. Traditionally, but not exclusively, this has applied to women seeking unavailable men. A woman *must* be sexy if even married men find her attractive, right? I mean, those guys can have sex whenever they want. Get real.

Our dear friend, John Gehrisch, who happens to be a PGA tour golfer, shared this gem with us… simply entitled "Christmas Golf." Want more gems? See the "Bimbo" companion book, "The Golf Pro Has Heart." He includes a Golf Gimme after each chapter. This one is designed purely for chuckles.

Four old timers were playing their weekly game of golf. One remarked how nice it would be to wake up on Christmas morning, roll out of bed, and, without an argument, go directly to the golf course, meet his buddies and play a round.

His cronies all chimed in and said, "Let's do it! We'll make it a priority. Figure out a way and meet here Christmas morning for our usual tee time."

The special morning arrived, and there they were on the golf course.

The first guy said, "Boy, this game cost me a fortune! I bought my wife a diamond ring that she can't take her eyes off."

The second guy said, "I spent a ton too. My wife is at home planning the cruise I gave her. She's up to her eyeballs in brochures."

The third guy said, "Well, my wife is at home admiring her new car, even reading the manual."

They all turned to the last guy in the group who was just staring at them like they'd lost their minds.

"I can't believe you all went to such expense for this golf game. I simply slapped my wife on the butt this morning and said, "Well babe, Merry Christmas! It's a great morning. Intercourse or the golf course?"

She said, "Don't forget your sweater!!!"

Oh, You're Married

Most people back off immediately when they learn a man or woman they have been flirting with is married, even if that married person initiated the flirtations. People "get it" that some married people tend to lie… a lot… about how sad their home life is. Or how poorly their spouse treats them. Or that they are separated or going through a divorce.

Further, most single people are sick of married people presenting themselves as both available and interested, when indeed they are merely "playing." Oh, yeah… and cheating. Gee, that is attractive. Not!

Others could not care less what someone's marital status might be.

Still others, find it particularly alluring to "capture" a married man or woman. Often this is just a power thing. Or a way of having fun, but avoiding commitment. Or a way to prevent getting close enough to let anyone hurt them. Or a way to feel "above" others of their own sex. The behavior is, indeed, *sexual* in nature, but far from *sexy*. The thrill for the cheater is fleeting, at best.

Through the Eyes of Babes

Sexy is sassy and fresh. Sexy is compelling, but not overbearing. Sexy is magnetic, yet genuinely innocent. Sexy is sensual, not sexual. I think sexy is like pornography, but only in the fact that it's difficult to define, although you "know it when you see it."

I remember going shopping with my youngest step-daughter and getting the opportunity to point out the difference between sensual or sexy and sexual.

As a young teen, she was feeling the need to both fit in and stand out. (Just one of the gazillion tortures of growing up.) Fashion choices are an extremely big part of how we portray ourselves and how we feel about ourselves.

Well, she was also an extremely smart and manipulative gal. I had to always pay very close attention. I'm glad I did. She often made me laugh right out loud.

That was the case on this one day when she was selecting new underwear during back-to-school shopping. After picking out a handful of the teeny-tiniest little string thongs, she turned to me and batted her eyelashes. Holding them up to me, she delivered her question in the most innocently sweet tones possible. "Aren't these cu-u-u-ute?!?"

With a choice of thousands of words, "cute" would not have ever have made the list. They were, however, overtly sexual. Of course, that was the obvious intent.

My little charge intended to wear them under jeans that would be pulled very low so every bit of "cheeky" sexuality and "butt floss" would be open for view.

"Come and get it!" That's what each pair screamed loud and clear. I knew it. *She* knew it. These would not pass this Evil Stepmother's scrutiny. I burst out laughing. Then, so did she.

In seriousness, part of a young teen's "right" is to push the envelope. But it's *our* responsibility to *push back*. She had to try. She certainly wasn't going to say to me, "Hey, aren't these sexy?" Even had she been that direct, she still would have gotten what she did… the sexual, <u>not</u> sensual… not sexy… explanation. And <u>no</u> tiny panties.

Further, I explained that sexy undies were not appropriate for a gal of her age. Heading off to high school, she could select attractive, feminine undies, but *not* for show to the boys. Certainly not thongs.

Tip: While it's not easy to be a parent or step-parent of kids "coming of age," it's vital to be the adult, even though this often puts undue stress on your loving relationship.

Section 8
THE LIES HAVE IT

29
<u>Sweet Little Lies</u>

> *"Always tell the truth.*
> *That way, you don't have to remember what you said."*
> -- Mark Twain (Samuel Clemens)(1835 – 1910)
> American author and humorist

I recall a Fleetwood Mac song by Christine McVie, imploring a lover to tell her sweet little lies. In real life, lies are rarely, if ever, sweet.

I'm not talking about "claiming the positive" here. For instance, I believe we should give ourselves positive self-talk. Claim the positive daily to help condition reality. Some examples could be:
- I will enjoy a peaceful, restful sleep tonight.
- I am getting healthier every day.
- I am developing better discipline and skills at work.

We'll talk more about affirmations later. This is not lying to yourself. You are claiming the positive. You are only lying to yourself if you claim something you are actively working against. So, if I say "I am getting healthier every day," I need to be taking diet and exercise steps to help make that a reality. If I am wolfing down a box of cupcakes, I am lying to myself.

I'm also not talking about socially polite etiquette. We've discussed this. Someone says, "Hi, how are you?" It's unlikely they actually want to know about the backache you woke up with this morning or the ongoing stress that has you feeling up to your eyeballs in alligators or the headache you're developing because you have been running around all day and forgot to eat.

A polite, "I'm fine, thank you" is typically expected. Is it a little white lie? I am afraid so, but it is on the passable list.

If the elderly hostess asks if you are having a nice time at her afternoon tea, I doubt she wants to hear that you can't wait to leave to go do something that is more fun.

A polite response is usually better than straight out bluntness, which can hurt someone's feelings or cause an unnecessary rift.

The opposite extreme would be acting so overly polite that you are seen as a "Pollyanna." That just means you express unrealistic optimism to a fault.

As with most things, balance is key. We do not want to lose our integrity and we do want to be sincere as much as possible. We simply want to be honest without unnecessarily hurting someone's feelings or stirring a misunderstanding.

If your husband smiles and tells you that you look beautiful, do not think of it as a sweet little lie. That's not taking anything away from the gorgeous ladies, such as Jennifer Anniston and Sandra Bullock, who have had magazines and fans name them "The Most Beautiful Woman in the World." When someone loves you, you truly <u>are</u> the most beautiful woman in the world to them. No lie.

There are, unfortunately, people in this world who've made a habit out of lying, and they lie to anyone at any time to further their own agendas. Some of these people are professional con artists, who knowingly victimize people with their lies. Some of these people lie when the truth would sound much better. It's not logical. It's hurtful and sick. These are self-centered people at best… sociopaths or pathological liars at worst.

Let Me Call You Sweetheart

Sam was traveling, but he called Susie, as usual, to tell her that he'd arrived safely at his destination. He said he was tired and turning in to watch television for the night.

She thought that that sounded odd since it was only 7 o'clock.

A couple hours later Sam texted to Susie a couple of times and mentioned a show he'd been watching and a sports score.

Susie called his hotel at 10 o'clock to say goodnight, only to discover that he had not yet checked in. She later learned he didn't get there until 1 o'clock in the morning.

Unfortunately, Susie saw the cell phone bill and learned that he'd traveled a great distance to another city before even placing his very first "I've arrived safely" phone call to her. The origination location of his text messages also revealed he was not in "his room" as he'd claimed, but in a town nearly an hour away.

Worse yet, after 11pm, the phone records showed a call to an unfamiliar phone number. It didn't take Susie much effort to research the number and learn it belonged to a strange woman, one who was completely beyond the scope of his visit. She was a "bar babe."

Susie was crushed. When he returned home, she asked Sam why he had told her that he was turning in early when he'd actually traveled elsewhere and stayed out so late.

Sam got angry.

"That's bullshit!" Sam bellowed. "After the tough day I'd had, how *dare* you!?!" He then stormed out of the room.

Okay, he'd gotten caught in his own web of deceit. So, gee, let's make it worse by getting all filled with feigned self-righteous indignation and trying to turn the tables on Susie, as if *she* was the one who'd screwed up.

It's like the little child who gets caught with his hand inside the cookie jar and crumbs all over his face who ends up yelling, "Why do you always pick on me? You always accuse *me*. I was only going to have just one!"

Adding more bull to bull yields bigger bull.

The best answer when we've hurt someone is never to hurt them *again*, even to save our *own* face. Susie had calmly shared her pain and confusion with Sam. He had broken her trust and confidence. Sam was the one who vowed to love and protect her. He was now the one who was hurting her.

Further phone records showed that Sam had indeed then shared various telephone and text conversations with the "other woman."

Susie asked Sam if he was unhappy with her… if she'd been letting him down in some way. His response revealed more about *him* than *her* as he yelled, "When you don't trust me, I can't stand you."

Seriously. Worse yet, it turned out that this was a repeating problem. Sam liked going out to bars and meeting women.

He didn't look at it as cheating, even when he carried on with someone else for months. His rationale was that he wasn't sleeping with anyone else but Susie, so he wasn't cheating.

I asked Susie what Sam would think if *she* went out to bars when he wasn't around, and met other men. No way! She didn't dare go anywhere when he was away. He would be livid, not to mention inconsolably jealous.

Naturally, he didn't want her out without him, since he presumed *she* would behave as *he* behaved. And he would *not* like it, nor tolerate it, if the shoe was on the other foot, so to speak.

I suggested she have that difficult conversation with him… "What's good for the gander is good for the goose" and all that. He needed to consider how he would feel if *she* behaved, even casually, in the same manner in which *he* behaved… especially if she was hiding it from him and getting angry at *him* when he found out and felt hurt.

Sam had never looked at his behavior that way. He acknowledged that he wouldn't stay with her. Yet, he was knowingly behaving badly, in the very same manner he would not tolerate.

That's sad, because now he had a long road back to earn Susie's trust again. His lies had been countless to Susie and to the other women, most of whom believed he was single or divorced… because that's what he'd told them.

Sam had taken Susie for granted in a most selfish and childish way. Oops! "Big mistake. Big. Huge." (I loved that line from the film "Pretty Woman.")

The last thing we want to do is to set our spouse up to be a vulnerable target for an affair with someone else who *does* show them respect and appreciation.

Direct lies, small lies, huge lies, and lies of omission… these are all self-serving and sources of self-destruction.

The perpetrator is also working to destroy the love relationship. If and when that comes to pass, the liar will very likely lie some more to make it appear that the wounded spouse was actually the liar, cheater, etc., etc., etc.

Tip: The truth is beautiful, even when it hurts.

30
<u>Truth in Living… Relationship Bending</u>

The one commonality in divorce is marriage.

Rodney was glad his wife, Sarah, didn't go out to bars or restaurants at night with the girls, because he didn't do "Boys Nights Out" either. He said that he'd see too many relationships spoiled from unplanned, but inevitable "monkey business." No problem, right? They agreed.

Yet, Sarah didn't understand. She felt repeatedly betrayed by his actions and words.

"I'm just running to the post office and Home Depot. Be right back," Rodney exclaimed, dashing out the door at 3pm.

By 7:30, she'd given up on him coming home for dinner. At 8 he waltzed in the door as if he'd only made those two errand stops. She knew better.

Still, he launched into telling her all about the long lines at the post office and his story of woes seeking and failing to find the one thing he needed at Home Depot.

He'd come home empty-handed and smelling of wine. The wine-stained teeth told Sarah all she needed to know. He'd been at a bar… and was now lying about it. Rodney continued rambling on about several people he'd happened to run into at the post office.

"Riiight," she thought.

However, this was far from the first time he'd repeated a similar scenario. She had learned to keep quiet. Previously, when she'd even hinted that it appeared he'd made one other stop for a beverage, he'd gone ballistic and started yelling at *her*.

Sharing Happy Hour had long been their special time together. Now Sarah couldn't help but wonder why she was excluded... and why Rodney felt he had to lie about it.

Truth in Living

People are interesting creatures. If someone *else* were to treat a friend of ours in a disrespectful manner, we would likely be livid, or at least highly disappointed in them. Our good instincts would call on us to defend and protect our friend. And yet, often without knowing it, we can treat our own dearest loved ones in a manner most unbefitting a person who cares.

It never ceases to amaze me how insensitive and insecure we humans tend to be. We can be very confident and self-assured on the outside, actively involved in our communities, successful and vibrant in our careers, and yet we are quivering jellyfish inside.

What do I mean by that?

Well, let's stay focused on relationships, for an example.

A man and woman can be absolutely committed to their marriage, and yet, one or the other partner can blow it up if they lack Truth in Living. They seek subtle or overt endorsements that they still have "it," making them attractive to others.

Though they would most likely deny it, they need regular or periodic reinforcement of their own desirability to others.

Too often, if one spouse or partner puts alcohol and mixed company together, they have set the stage for potential disaster. If we build a friendship with a member of the opposite sex... a friendship that does not equally involve the spouse or relative spouses... it's just a matter of time before fireworks will launch in the vast majority of cases.

You need not involve alcohol or bars either. Marriage counselors will tell you that this scenario rings most frequently in our work environments, where men and women now work more closely than in any other time in our history.

Day-to-day conversations can easily evolve to working lunches and friendships and then social lunches and then catching a drink after work, etc. The new "friend" ends up getting more of the personal verbal and emotional "sharing" than the spouse.

A spouse usually senses they are being increasingly shut out; their lover is paying them less and less attention. The "busy" partner typically tells the questioning spouse that they are being overly sensitive, overreacting, being jealous, or being foolish.
Or they try to validate their activities as just a normal part of their stressful career environment.

Success Recipe

What they need to do is flirt. Send love notes. Zip off a few jazzy emails. Leave some sexy phone messages. Date. Date often. Plan some extra special dates. And be *sure* that ALL these above mentioned activities are with their *own* spouse only.

My husband always jokes about this. After we got married, he'd quip that I wouldn't let him date any more.

I'd always correct him that, of course he can date. In fact, he'd better be dating... ME.

We developed a sassy "bit" that sometimes he was out with his wife, and sometimes he was out with his girlfriend. I get the lucky role of both wife and girlfriend.

Now... put all kidding aside. If we encourage social meetings with someone other than our partner, we are literally loading explosives under our own love relationship.

If we do anything to invite future conversations or meetings with an outside person, say someone we just met… such as sharing cell phone numbers or business cards (when there really is not even a façade of a business relationship), then we've added even *more* dynamite.

We should never even hint that we look forward to "seeing" this person again sometime. If we do, we have actually LIT THE FUSES that could destroy our marriage or loving relationship.

Imagine the destruction of trust and respect that actually meeting that new person again will cause if the person you love ever found out??!!? Believe it or not, they will.

And denial doesn't work. Then your spouse knows that you are a deliberate liar as well as a cheater. Bad combination; bad decision.

Now, if we cross the line of physical intimacy with that new person, we've gone way beyond breaking trust with our spouse or partner. We have actively and knowingly blown up and destroyed our relationship.

If it was ever actually important to us, the responsibility is 1000% on our own shoulders to try and rebuild and restore trust and respect again… trust and respect that we've proven we do not deserve.

How easy it is in this "modern" day thinking to say that there is no hurt caused or damage done if our spouse or partner doesn't <u>know</u> that we've chatted in person or by phone or online with someone else.

Oh, really?!!? Remember, *that* time-worn rationalization is wrong on all counts.

The damage is violent, because we are exhibiting complete disrespect for a very important person.

Mixed Company Messages

How DO we deal with these mixed company social situations where someone offers us their card or number and suggests getting together or talking again?

We could enthusiastically say it would be great AND include that your lover, spouse, or partner will enjoy meeting them. That will make it perfectly clear that you are not "in the market" for a new love or special "friend."

If we are not strong and true enough people to have already made it very clear that we have and are happy with a committed relationship, we better at least have the guts to turn down any business card offers.

Okay, look at the card and be gracious. But upon departure, make it clear to the "new" party that you are NOT taking the card with you.

Don't give me any guff about *that* being disrespectful to this new person. We should worry about being respectful to the person we love and leave the card behind in an obvious manner.

Seriously, we know if we're screwing up in a relationship in this manner. For me it's always been easy to simply think, "If my husband suddenly appeared, would he approve of what I am doing or saying… or could it appear disrespectful of him and our love?"

Or, I can consider what *I* would think if my spouse was doing something that I am doing. If it would be AOK with me, then I'm probably not crossing any line. If there is any question, however, I should run – not walk – to the nearest exit and get my act together.

'Nuff said.

31
<u>Volume Control</u>

Work out your anger so you won't *take* out your anger on anyone.

Anger is a weird beast. Some people are quick to anger. Others are slow to anger. Regardless, if we get frustrated enough, we get angry.

What we do when we are angry is a personal decision. Some people allow themselves to rant and rave, yell and swear, throw things or throw punches. They typically do this under the guise of their behavior being the fault of someone else. It is not. It is 100% their own fault AND 100% within their own control.

It matters little whether they grew up observing adults behaving poorly when angry or if they developed these behaviors as an adult to force people to give them their way. What we do in anger is rarely good.

When angry, our volume levels go up, up, up! That is also a bad choice. It's said that we do this to cover the chasm of space that has been created between the two people due to the anger. You could be standing face to face with an angry person, but you might as well be a hundred yards away.

Some people believe that if they yell and scream, others will get the point of just how serious they are. For me, all I get is the point of just how out of control that someone is.

Steve and Lanie seemed to be fighting more than they were <u>not</u> fighting. They claimed to be madly in love with each other. They believed vehemently that they were each other's soul mate.

However, from the outside, it seemed that they were not good for each other. Once they'd get together for a week or so, they'd be fighting… again… and ultimately break up.

We lost track of how many times they'd broken up. Each time they got back together again, Lanie would say that Steve only got so angry because he loved her so much. She'd never felt that anyone had ever cared about her that much.

I personally wondered how she could be even thinking of marrying him, when they repeatedly screamed at each other and broke up. To boot, each time they broke up, whether it was for a couple of weeks or a couple of months, they'd both start dating someone else.

To me, this was not love. Lust, maybe. They shared an extreme attraction, but it was not a healthy one to my way of thinking. I would want to run far away.

I often suggest in a relationship, that when we are going to argue, we should only do so while holding hands. That may sound strange. I agree, because the last thing you *want* to do with someone with whom you are angry is hold their hands.

And yet, when holding *both* of their hands, we are compelled to look each other in the eyes.

We cannot feel the raging distance that anger traditionally interjects. We are more apt to keep our volume under control.

If someone yells at me, they are not expressing love. They may be threatening me. They may be expressing great frustration with me. They may simply be trying to control my behavior. However, they are not communicating love.

Actually, when we resort to screaming at someone, we are revealing weakness and a sense of helplessness. If we can't seem to get our message or feelings across any other way, then we get angry, and we get loud!

One of the greatest skills I developed in this area is the ability to *NOT* go toe-to-toe with a screamer. Because our communication efforts have broken down, I need not break down with them.

This is not to say that the screaming person is not *hurting* me. Their nasty rantings are extraordinarily painful. However, releasing anger by exploding at someone is not the best way to communicate, never mind to get someone to do what we wish they would do. For me, in fact, it is the opposite.

Let's say that I was about to start folding the clean laundry. My spouse starts yelling and screaming at me for being a lousy, good-for-nothing idiot who can't even get the laundry done. Well, surprise. Now, I couldn't care less if I fold their laundry.

Depending on just how nasty they were to me, I might just walk away. Or I might fold *our* items such as towels and my personal items, and leave their personal items unfolded. Yup, that is spiteful. But if someone yells at me, it makes me want to do the opposite of what they want.

"Pobody's Nerfect." (Yes, that's a deliberate typo or "mord wixing" of "Nobody's Perfect.")

In all honesty, my first reaction when someone starts to yell is to try to defuse the situation. Sometimes an understanding comment or even a smidgeon of light humor is all it takes. Sometimes there is absolutely *nothing* that can be said or done to get the screamer off their mountaintop.

Now, I have not always had a calm reaction. In fact, I screamed someone down in no uncertain terms once. I'm none too proud of it. It was during college.

I no longer even remember why, but a fellow student had yelled at a couple of gals to the point where they were in tears. In fight or flight scenarios, I am all about flight. But on this occasion, I knew he was no match in wits for me, and I took him down… without mercy.

I was loud. I was hurtful. I was awful. I have never forgotten what I did. It was tough to forgive myself for it, and I have never repeated it.

Learning to control our anger is possible. It's also a very constructive skill to develop.

Some children did not get to learn this because they heard a lot of yelling in their home. Kids can grow up thinking that yelling is a natural and normal manner of communication.

Sorry, but if you're yelling at me, it better be to save my life from an oncoming truck or something. Everyone who learned to *yell* can also learn to *not* yell… and become a more effective communicator as a result.

Loud Lies

That said, when you are dealing with a liar, you will probably also be dealing with a yeller. Liars often think it makes their point more valid if they say it at the top of their lungs or in an angrily snarling tone.

I suppose that if they spoke at a normal conversational volume level, it would be more difficult for them to rationalize their lies. Logic coming back at them in a two-way conversation, often inspires them to get louder. They can't win their point with conversation, so they turn up the volume to try and scream reality away.

Screaming and repeating lies makes them neither true nor more believable.

In fact, yelling to get our point across lowers our credibility. If I have to scream to get you to listen to me, I just may not have something worthy to say. This is the problem with liars (and other strangers). And if someone is yelling at you, feel free to make them a stranger.

Get Healthy

In a relationship, yelling is most frequently used as a means of exuding power and control. The one being yelled at is often squashed into silence. This is not due to logic nor agreement. This is the result of fear. This is not healthy.

If partners yell at each other over touchy issues, it will quickly become desirable to avoid bringing up such issues. This is not healthy.

If someone is yelling at their spouse, it shows a certain helplessness on the screamer's part. They are revealing that they do not possess the confidence or conversational skills to make their point or express an opinion. This is not healthy.

If someone yells as a reaction to something that has happened, they are displaying a quick emotional flashpoint… a short fuse. This is not healthy.

Scenarios such as these can go on and on. But if we step back, we *can* find healthy ways to avoid yelling.

No relationship should be based on control and fear. If yelling is happening in your relationship, professional help may be beneficial to find a level of mutual trust and respect. Yelling to laud over someone else is not productive nor positive.

If there _is_ yelling when trying to discuss sensitive issues, improved conversational skills can save the relationship. Start by discussing a less controversial issue.

Understand that there *is* more than one right way to accomplish something, and *both* parties' viewpoints are equally valid.

Once you can talk calmly and respectfully about simple issues, move forward to larger issues. Just keep it calm, quiet, and respectful.

If one partner has difficulty expressing themselves, it could help to schedule a topic for discussion. This allows the less communicative partner time to jot down a few points that may be important to them. Once in a conversation, they then won't "freeze" with nothing to say. They will have their notes.

A short fuse derails communication. This makes the other partner feel that icky sense of "always walking on eggshells."

The yeller needs to be encouraged to react openly, but not loudly. If they get loud, call for a timeout. Why not? Just take a few minutes. Come back in ten to thirty minutes and try again.

Keep all eggshells in the carton and not underfoot.

<u>Super Tips</u>

My way of responding to someone yelling at me is to speak more softly. I've said it before, and I'll say it again and again. I choose *not* to go toe-to-toe with a screamer. There is no gain.

Picture the fight. He kicks it off with a screaming accusation. She kicks it up a notch by screaming right back. He goes up another notch by leaning into her face and yelling. Up one more tick as she continues yelling and wags her finger in his face. This goes on and on, with no victor. There's just yelling, name calling, and rage.

Re-picture the same fight. He kicks it off with a screaming accusation. She neutralizes his anger by calmly asking if he'd like to sit down and talk about it. He yells, "There's nothing to talk about because you're a f#$*ing bitch!"

She softly responds that she is glad to talk with him, but only when he calms down.

Whether he chooses to simmer down quickly or slowly, she has made the positively assertive stand that conversation will be calm or it won't happen.

Again, call for a timeout. This is perfectly acceptable, even if one of the partners doesn't want to stop fighting. A timeout is healthy. It allows time to calm down.

Take yelling at each other in anger off the table. It's not positive to yell at each other. We can *tell* each other that we are hurt, angry, or frustrated. Yelling is counterproductive.

If one person yells, do not yell back.

My Mom's control used to drive me crazy as a kid. When she wanted to yell, she would just start counting out loud instead.

"One, two, three, four, five, six, seven, eight, nine, ten." Sometimes she would count to ten several times, depending just how "ticked off" I had her. She is one very smart woman.

Try not to criticize the person yelling. Even if they are calling you names or swearing as part of their ranting, don't play their game. Talk calmly and evenly.

If either of you has been drinking alcohol, suggest the conversation will be more productive and on target if you start again when both of you are completely sober.

Always make it calmly clear that yelling is not *ever* part of the solution.

Without making accusations, be sure to share how the yelling is making you feel. It is difficult if not impossible to have constructive conversations when an out-of-control volume level is intimidating or overwhelming you.

Let your partner know that you truly and sincerely want to hear what they are trying to say, but make it clear that yelling cannot be part of the expression.

By the way, if you are in a situation where a spouse yells at you, especially with angry name calling and vicious, hateful faces, this is indeed abuse. It should *not* be tolerated. Offenders rarely, if ever, recognize that they are at fault for their offenses. So, perhaps most important of all is to stay safe.

If the person yelling is putting you in danger, you best step away. Protect yourself. Get outside help if you need it.

I opened the book with a reflection on a documentary I produced and hosted was about domestic violence. The program sub-title, "When Home Is No Haven," said it all, because your home *should* be a safe place.

Unfortunately, for far too many people, home often erupts into a violent battlefield. Interviewing survivors was most humbling and moving. Again, I will never forget the feeling of "There, but for the Grace of God, go I."

No matter where you are, help is available 24/7. If the situation is dire, dial 911.

The National Domestic Violence Hotline
www.TheHotline.org
1-800-799-SAFE (7233)

Also see:
www.DomesticShelters.org

Tip: When communication breaks down, don't break down with it.

32
<u>Serial Liars</u>

Getting laid and getting lied to are ridiculously similar. Just as getting laid is not like making love, getting lied to is only good for the liar.

If you live with and love a liar or a cheater, you have to figure out what keeps you in the relationship. Sometimes it's because they've depleted your financial resources, or you feel too old to start over, or you lack self-confidence, or they keep insisting that it's all in your head (and you desperately want to believe them).

Other times it's because, despite their shortcomings, you are best friends, and neither of you want to lose each other. You may have great fun together or feel stronger together as a couple than apart. You may truly be in love, though the misbehaving partner is a total sham when it comes to loyalty.

Most importantly, **do *not* blame yourself**.

Let me tell you about Samantha, Sam for short. She is a beautiful, smart, talented, and hard-working woman. Her vivacious personality, wit, and positive attitude make her a complete joy to be around.

Her husband is gregarious, with a magnetic persona, making him very popular with all their friends. Unfortunately, Joe is also a serial liar.

Interestingly, Joe says that he hates being lied to, and he insists that he would never lie, especially not to Samantha. Then he gets frustrated because he does it again… and again. Worse yet, Joe says that he feels aghast and angry when any of his lies get pointed out to him. Still, he just can't help himself.

Once, he admitted that he turned on the home security system but only activated the doors. He said that he knew Samantha, who was at her parents' home caring for her sick mother, would look online and believe that he was at home because he'd called her at 4:30 to tell her that he was exhausted and was going to take a nap. Then Joe had climbed out a first floor window to make it appear that he was still home, while he actually scurried off to a local bar.

Sam knew his phone call about taking a nap at 4:30 was most likely bogus. Sure enough, the bedroom motion detectors went silent within 2 minutes of his phone call and weren't triggered again until well after 9pm.

Samantha realized that Joe forgot that the bedroom motion detector picks up even when he rolls over or uses the TV's remote control. And he never took a nap nor tried to go to sleep without watching television.

So, why the lies? It made no sense to Sam. She loved him, and had decided to recognize that his behavior pattern likely stemmed from some point in his past.

Now he couldn't control himself. She'd even pleaded with him to simply trust her and to be honest with her. Instead, she continually learned from other people that Joe had been in various places other than wherever he'd said he was. Though she stopped feeling like a fool, she could not shake the reality that she could not trust the man she loved.

Sometimes, when she explained how much it hurt her to learn that he'd been out, carrying on in a bar and even flirting rather strongly with another woman, he apologized, but only *after* getting angry *first*. He then begged her forgiveness and promised it would never happen again. He did not want to lose her.

Was he truly remorseful? Had he actually turned over a new leaf? Nope. He still liked "doing his own thing," and lying to her. If he could only imagine how demeaning it would feel if *she* were doing these sneaky things and repeatedly lying to *him*.

It's like the hot shot athletes, movie stars, or politicos who get caught cheating on a spouse or with their hand in some other "cookie jar." Suddenly they are full of apologies and remorse.

Helllloooo! They are ONLY sorry that they got *caught*. Had their faux pas not gone public, they would have continued down their self-centered, hurtful, harmful paths.

I know a great number of strong, beautiful, and highly talented women who are in long-term relationships with men who do not behave well. These women may think they are with men, but they are merely with males.

Some of these males likely see themselves as true Casanova's. These guys look good, offer engaging personalities, and are fun to be around. It matters not how well-loved a self-dubbed Casanova is. He always has the "roving eye" and jumps at "new conquest" opportunities. He offers little regard for loved ones getting hurt, as long as he is getting what *he* wants. These guys... notice I cannot call them "men"... are simply childish, undisciplined frauds... most *un*appealing character traits.

Okay, it's true. There *are* Casanova-type females as well, though they are far less common. However, both males and females can present as chronic liars, serial cheaters, and porn freaks, as well as abusers via other physical, verbal, and psychological means.

Sure, opposites attract, but I believe that great people deserve to be with other great people. It is sad when wonderful people love someone who brings so much inner (and outer) sadness to the relationship. Siiigh.

> *"I guess sometimes we overlook the obvious,*
> *because we love someone*
> *and we want to believe the best."*
>
> -- John A. Gehrisch (1947 -)
> American Entrepreneur and Tour Golf Professional

Frustrating is the only way to describe how it feels to be lied to regularly, especially by someone we love. There's nothing logical going on, so don't look for a logical reason. In fact, serial liars actually lie, exaggerate, and "pontificate" to anyone and everyone about virtually anything and everything.

Thus, the injured partner should not take the liar's issues personally. They are not being singled out for the bad behavior.

That said, it doesn't make it confuse or hurt any less.

Living with a liar is beyond challenging. Their deceptions can throw us completely off balance. We get accustomed to the liar deflecting questions, misplacing blame, and wreaking emotional havoc.

That said, remember there are "little white lies," half-truths, and stretched stories and exaggerations. We need to consciously learn to live with integrity.

All people lie, but *some* people are liars.

Liars are highly unlikely to admit their lies, never mind apologize for the hurt they've caused. Liars don't genuinely apologize. Deceit has become their full-out lifestyle. They are centered on themselves with no thoughts of the consequences of their lies.

In cowardly style, they tell more lies to try and cover their tracks. They are not good at admitting they actually have shortcomings.

There is tremendous trauma in the betrayal caused by a perpetual liar as they repeatedly commit psychological abuse. If you've lived with a liar, you know how this feels.

The liar delivers false information with vehement insistence that the lies are truths, pushing their victims to question their own good judgment, memory, and even facts of reality.

You are not delusional, but a polished liar can make you think you may be at times. If you remember the old movie, "Gaslight," you understand what I mean when I say a liar can drive you nutty.

In truth, you are not the problem. It's highly unlikely that you have emotional and psychological instability.

You are not weak-willed. You are not paranoid. You are human. Someone has taken advantage of your vulnerability. They've burned you!

As the victim of a liar, you have suffered a debilitating trauma. Don't hesitate to get some support through a therapist or even as part of a trauma support group. You have been "gaslighted."

As an expert who writes on the topic, Dr. Robert Weiss reminds victims that they can become "wiser, stronger, and willing to once again risk vulnerability in the name of love and intimate connection."

Tip: Liars feel justified in telling and living with their lies. *They are not.*

Section 9
YOUR CHEATING HEART

33
<u>Dissing the Dame</u>

> *"It may sound ordinary for a woman*
> *to find out her husband is cheating on her,*
> *but not if you are the woman, and it's your husband."*
> -- Melissa Bank (1961 -)
> American author

Don't think for a minute that affairs only happen in unhappy marriages. Don't think they only happen in marriages where the couple isn't sharing plenty of sex together. Don't think they only happen in marriages where the couple doesn't talk or share intellectual intimacy any longer.

Affairs happen in marriages where one partner needs outside ego boosting. Affairs happen in marriages where one partner has not made a true commitment and may not be capable of it. Affairs happen in marriages where one or both partners get lazy.

Cheating can become a regular part of one partner's activity to one degree or another. They can get to the point where they convince themselves they aren't even doing something wrong. They rarely, if ever, use the word "cheating" in relation to what they are doing outside their marriage or committed relationship.

> *"You are not ashamed of your sin in committing adultery because so many men commit it. Man's wickedness is now such that men are more ashamed of chastity than of lechery. Those who sleep with his servant girl in brazen lechery is liked and admired for it, and people make light of the damage to his soul. If any man has the nerve to say that he is faithful to his wife, other men will mock him and despise him and say he's not a real man, for man's wickedness is now of such proportions that no man is considered a man unless he is overcome by lechery."*
> - Augustine of Hippo
> Sermons 1-19

If your partner is a cheater, a player, or philanderer by any other words, you are apt to catch on to their M.O. or Modus Operandi. They will have patterns. Often they start treating their partner differently, either negatively or positively. They may get extra sweet or extra nasty for no obvious reason. These are some of the things that make us say, "Hmmmmm."

Another standard is, if you are out together, be aware if they make a point of "putting down" some other party. Often this is purely for your benefit. Call it a smoke screen. For example, your lover regularly says a particular woman is ugly or mean. He adds more, saying he can't imagine anyone putting up with her.

Okay, he says it once or twice, no big deal. However, if he makes this a regular diatribe or regularly brings up her name, beware. This should make you say, "Hmmmmm."

Especially take warning if he comes up with a negative nickname, such as "Frog Face" or "Pass Around Pack"… anything derogatory. These steps are meant to further enforce his supposed *lack* of interest. Naturally, he says none of his dribble in front of *her*. Take notice when she's around if he moves close to her, smiling and laughing. If they appear to share some inside joke, you are toast.

One lovely gal even saw her husband pat "the other woman" on the bum as he "conveniently" walked past her. Then he vehemently denied having done what he'd literally been caught doing. Please!

A quick check of phone records revealed there had been lots of recent phone and text message exchanges. Of course, the cheater had a logical, "business" explanation… he just forgot to mention that the "business" was monkey business.

If we love someone, we must never cheat.

Cheating is pure hypocrisy. Our partner deserves better than that. If we don't love someone, we should not be with them. That would also be hypocrisy.

Then again, I've heard it said that to be faithful to someone you don't love is hypocrisy to yourself. Actually, I don't think that is possible, for if you are faithful to someone, your actions show your love for them. People are typically not faithful to someone they don't love. There is no need nor desire to be. Cheating shows people's love for themselves. They are showing total disregard for everyone else.

Remember North Carolina's former U.S. Senator John Edwards, a man who wanted to be President? It was eventually reported that he'd begun an extramarital affair in 2007, if not earlier. He was initially running for President, and then had hoped to become Barack Obama's vice-presidential running mate. All political aspirations, along with positive public sentiment, evaporated. Rumors emerged that he had promised the girlfriend that he'd marry her once his wife, Elizabeth, was out of the picture.

Elizabeth had been going through a heinous battle with breast cancer. When she was in remission, late in 2008, he admitted the affair, but denied he was the father of the baby his mistress had delivered. Then, to add insult to injury, he continued the affair, even after Elizabeth's cancer returned and was declared incurable. In January, 2010, John Edwards finally admitted that he was indeed the father of the baby. He and his ailing wife separated.

While he had tried to present himself as an ideal husband and father, a true public servant of the people and the working man, he revealed himself to be another ego-centric cheater who fathered a child with another woman while his wife was fighting for her life due to breast cancer. Elizabeth Edwards died in December, 2010.

We see this pattern of public figures denying all improprieties over and over again, until so many sources reveal information that the scoundrels are forced into an admission.

Just because there is a high level of celebrity should *not* mean there is a low level of personal integrity.

However, the American public seems to have grown numb to the constant parade of political sex scandals. We want better, but we seem to keep accepting that politicians are scoundrels on most fronts. Why should sex or honesty be any different?

President Bill Clinton was impeached for perjury and obstruction of justice. Though not the reason for the impeachment, he lied under oath about his affair with Monica Lewinsky. Though he initially tried vehemently to deny having ever "had sex with that woman," it was just one his *many* extra-marital sex scandal allegations.

President Thomas Jefferson was noted for fathering the children of one of his slaves. U.S. Senator Daniel Webster was also alleged to have had several mistresses.

President Warren Harding was said to have had two mistresses, one of which produced a daughter while Harding was still a U.S. Senator.

President John F. Kennedy's extramarital dalliances have been chronicled numerous times, including the famously alleged relationship with Marilyn Monroe. His VP and successor, Lyndon Johnson, was apparently far worse and frequently acknowledged as horribly foul-mouthed, too.

Extra-marital affairs blanket all levels of public service. For example, many women are said to have had scandalous liaisons with U.S. Supreme Court Justice William O. Douglas.

Four-star General David Petraeus was named Director of the CIA until his adultery came to light.

New York Governor Eliot Spitzer got caught hiring prostitutes with misappropriated funds no less.

Though South Carolina Governor Mark Sanford told his wife that he was hiking the Appalachian Trail, he'd actually disappeared for days to visit his mistress in Argentina.

Various Congressmen have had sexual misconduct woes, including President Kennedy's brother Ted. Unapologetically, U.S. Senator Edward Kennedy didn't even attempt to mask most of his affairs.

Perhaps the most notorious was Senator Gary Hart. While seeking the Democratic nomination for President, he brazenly challenged the media to follow him if they wanted proof of his marital loyalty. They did and photographed him traveling in the Bahamas with model Donna Rice on a boat named "Monkey Business." Perfect.

Whether it involves interns or staffers, having children out of wedlock, sexting, facing multiple charges of sexual harassment, or a wide variety of other sex scandals, many political leaders seem to believe they are "above it all," as if they were somehow entitled to do as they please sexually. There seems little or no regard for wives nor their target victims.

Many of these cheaters had also taken great pride and pleasure in pointing the accusatory finger at *other* offenders… until their *own* improprieties and misdeeds surfaced, that is.

Then there are relationships that cross over between political power and Hollywood celebrity. For example, in 2011, Maria Shriver and Arnold Schwarzenegger ended their 25-year-marriage, after he'd fathered a child with the family's long-time cleaning woman. That child had become a teenager before the truth was revealed.

Hollywood affairs are legendary, along with the breakups they cause. Among the more famous is the 1959 divorce of Debbie Reynolds and Eddie Fisher. The couple had only been married for four years, but he'd fallen for Elizabeth Taylor.

In 2001, Meg Ryan and Dennis Quaid divorced after a 9-year marriage, due to an extra-marital relationship she had started with Russell Crowe on a movie set the previous year.

In 2005, Brad Pitt ended his 4-year relationship with Jennifer Aniston to be with Angelina Jolie, with whom he had become involved while they worked on the film "Mr. and Mrs. Smith."

In 2010, Sandra Bullock divorced Jesse James, her husband of less than five years, after various women announced affairs with James.

Movie stars are far from the most notorious cheaters. From rock stars to pro athletes, some people literally throw themselves at celebrities… and the celebrities throw themselves right back, often throwing away marriages and families. The affairs of professional athletes are ridiculously legendary.

In 2009, Tiger Woods' marriage to Swedish model Elin Nordegren exploded when his long list of mistresses and misdeeds started coming to light. He's far from the only athlete to get caught.

The NFL has long lists of cheaters, from Tiki Barber losing his beautiful wife due to an affair with a TV intern to the New York Jets' Mark Gastineau having an affair and a child with Brigette Nielsen while he was still married.

Baseball is fraught with extra-marital flings, too. Johnny Damon bragged about his numerous cheating episodes, and Barry Bonds actually continued an ongoing affair for several years following the wedding to his second wife.

Paul LoDuca lost his Playboy model wife when his affair with a college student came to light.

Roger Clemens' marriage endured several alleged affairs, but Alex Rodriguez' wife filed for divorce after his numerous dalliances with strippers, hookers, and, reportedly, anyone else.

The NBA has seen more than its share of ridiculous offenders. Michael Jordan, Shaquille O'Neal, and Jason Kidd are all among those who lost their marriages due to multiple infidelities.

Cheating cost Tony Parker his marriage to the celebrated beauty Eva Longoria, and the Miami Heat's Dwyanne Wade had affairs on the woman with whom he was having an affair, despite having a sensationally gorgeous wife.

Then, of course, there's the L.A. Laker's Kobe Bryant. His wife believes in standing by her man, despite the fact that his alleged sexual exploits came to light and blasted his prior reputation out of the water as one of "the good guys."

Personally, I think people in high profile positions should be held to a higher standard of conduct. They are visible role models and opinion leaders. I am wearied by the excuses and apologies to spouses and hurt loved ones each time they are caught. How about living up to the positive role model image they seek to portray?

Men have been wronged by women, too. I know that. However, statistics show that men still hold the torch far above the numbers of cheating women. That doesn't make the pain caused any less viable or the offending women any less responsible.

Remember, it takes two to tango. Offenders are not just the cheaters. Offenders are also those who engage in the affair with someone they know is cheating.

Let me tell you Rissy and Roland's story. They had a fairy tale romance. After they became engaged to be married, Roland confessed that he had an affair when he was married previously. He promised it would never happen again. Rissy loved and believed him. He was a gentleman and a gentle man.

They had a loving marriage. After his aging mother's home burned down, and she was widowed, Rissy had moved her in with them and lovingly cared for her. She also had nursed Roland himself back to health following his heart attack. They worked hard, but they had a laughter-filled time and never seemed to even argue.

Still, after 7 years of marriage, they divorced. Roland begged for her to reconsider her decision. Unfortunately, he had not been able to have sex with her for 6½ years. He blamed his cigarette smoking for his squelched libido. He wouldn't quit smoking.

Rissy felt guilty divorcing him, but she felt too young to just give up on ever having sex again.

They'd had a fabulous sex life before marriage. Yet, she could still remember the first night he got a "headache." They'd laughed that it was supposed to be the wife claiming that.

Shortly after their divorce, Rissy came across a large collection of graphic correspondence that he'd saved. It revealed that he'd started cheating on her just six months after they'd gotten married. It was a gal from his office… Shockeroo… also a wedding guest.

When returning some of his belongings to him, she told Roland that it was hurtful of him to have let her feel guilty for divorcing him, when he knew full well he'd been cheating on her for so long. Now it even turned out that he'd had the heart attack on the eve of a time he believed a mistress was about to blow the whistle on him.

Rissy asked Roland how long *he'd* have put up with no sex had the situation been reversed. He honestly replied, "About 6 months."

"Well," she said. "Call me 6 years stupid."

Rissy learned that he'd had unresolved childhood issues that made it virtually impossible for him to have sex with his wife. Roland had placed her on a pedestal. To him, sex was dirty. This was why he'd cheated on his first wife, too. He learned he needed help too late to save his marriage to anyone.

Extra-marital affairs become things of legend… and often the undoing of legends… and mere mortals.

Tip: If there are unresolved issues, don't put on blinders. Get help.

34
<u>Heard It Through the Grapevine</u>

Marvin Gaye recorded a hit song about learning through the grapevine that he was losing his lover. "I Heard It Through the Grapevine" was written by Norma Whitfield and Barrett Strong in 1966, back when the grapevine was woven of whispers passed behind our backs… and then passed on and on and on to and through others.

Today's grapevine is dramatically larger and faster than ever before in history. Many factors contribute to that fact, from the commonality of cell phones and texting to the preponderance of emails and social media.

Gossip and rumors travel fast. They do not express opinions. They allege factual information. Unfortunately, they are most often negative.

That fact reflects the negative side of human nature. We see this most often with regard to politicians and celebrities. We humans are an envious lot. We like dirt. We take a certain perverse pleasure in trying to put or pull successful or celebrated people down a few pegs.

Before I first went to work in a local television station, I literally turned them down three times. I'd grown up in the area. People laughed openly at what was deemed to be an amateurish newscast. No way could I be seen on the news. What would I tell my friends?

Oh, yeah. I was quite the know-it-all little snot. In truth, I knew nothing.

The General Manager insisted that he and the station's new ownership were going to turn it into a "real" station.

To appease my desire to not be associated with the news operation, he literally created for me what I soon learned was a non-existent job. My first official title was Special Projects Coordinator.

Riiight. Week one, however, he had me out doing news interviews, stories and live reports, in addition to starting work on documentaries and specials that I would produce and host.

I soon learned of some laughter at my expense in the news department. A copy of my resume had found its way into a couple of reporters' hands. My marketing and theatrical background stirred lots of snickering, at best.

Hmmm… What goes around comes around. I deserved it. We were all young and goofy. I needed to earn "my stripes."

Okay. I had long hair… at a time when female newscasters did not. I didn't dress in traditional blazers and petite jewelry. I didn't have any educational or career background in journalism or broadcasting.

These co-workers did not know that the new management had seen me hosting a live Easter Seals telethon, perceived what they saw as capabilities in this local businesswoman, and tracked me down. Some just saw that a bimbo had arrived on the scene and was garnering a lot of attention. Thus the rumor mill cranked.

"She must be sleeping with the General Manager."

Quite frankly, I was surprised. I did not see myself as any threat to my co-workers. I was simply doing my job. Perhaps I should say that I was learning to do my job. And I had to learn it ALL, which I did hungrily. I worked hard to earn my co-workers' respect.

It turned out that the GM was determined to make me an award-winning lead news anchor. And he did.

We broke ground and broke records. It was fun to be part of a team taking the station from worst to first in the ABC fleet of affiliates.

The General Manager had hired me. The News Director admittedly got no say in the matter. The same GM, David Zamichow, remains to this day the absolute toughest *and* best boss I ever had. He seemed to know everybody's job and pushed us all to get the very best out of each of us.

We wanted to succeed, but when we let him down, I thought he'd pop a vein. I remember him tersely saying things like, "And what do you think you could have done differently in this situation?"

Gulp. And we did better next time.

You could talk with Mr. Z about anything… even rumors, gossips, and negative critics. I remember him telling me, "Get strong. In this field or any other, the higher you go the more sharks will be circling." He remains a very wise man.

I found his sage remarks held true in personal relationships, too. I find it sad that there are those people who *want* to see happy people and happy couples fail. Sad, but true. There is a lot of envy out there. A lot of jealousy. A lot of bitterness and anger. A lot of self-loathing and self-doubt. A lot of frustration.

When people believe they will be happier if they can put someone else down, they are wrong.

We are happier when we help *others* be happier and grow to become the best *they* can be.

We need not leap to negative assumptions about others. We shouldn't get involved in spreading vicious gossip or baseless rumors. We all need to separate rumors and gossip from reality.

That said, with cameras seemingly everywhere, along with highly pervasive social media outlets on the rise, secrets come out.

Today's grapevine does not reflect mere rumor and gossip. Now it comes complete with photographs, eye witness accounts, and hard evidence. These information factoids fly at lightning speed through sites like Twitter, Facebook, and Instagram.

It's impossible to count the number of people whose attempts to sneak around, cheat, lie, or falsely represent themselves as single or available have been thwarted or revealed by sites like Facebook. Today we can simply "Google" someone's name and come up with loads of information and photographs.

In today's social scene, especially the dating scene, be very wary of someone who says that they don't use Facebook, email, a cell phone, etc. They may well lie about other things too.

Really savvy liars even have a second cell phone, just for "liaisons." Call it a burner phone, a throw-away phone, or simply a pre-paid phone for which they keep a second account, hidden from the spouse at home.

When someone trying to socialize with you says they don't use social media, try Googling their name. See what you can learn.

There's usually a good reason they are trying to lead you away from seeking them on social media. For instance, you are apt to learn that they are married or in a committed relationship.

Nope, Not Me

Also, remember that a rumor is only a rumor because it's unverified information. Once verified as factual, it's no longer a rumor. It's not hearsay. It's factual.

Regardless, there will still be people who will deny, deny, deny reality… as if denying it will make it less true. This remains the case whether we're looking at cheaters or politicians. (But wait! I repeat myself.)

"We are not about to send our American boys 9- or 10-thousand miles away from home to do what Asian boys should be doing for themselves."
"I am not a crook."
"Cigarette smoking is no more addictive than coffee, tea, or Twinkies."
"Read my lips. No new taxes."
"I did not have sex with that woman."
"I invented the Internet."
"The Keystone XL pipeline bypasses the United States."
"I did not knowingly receive or send any classified material on my private email server."
"If you like the health care plan you currently have, you can keep it."
"The Affordable Health Care Act provided coverage to 129 million people who would have otherwise been denied coverage."

Okay, enough of the political malarkey. Both sides of the aisle make us sick with guff.

Lovers are no strangers to the "lies that blind" either.

"I'm stuck in traffic."
"I'm not jealous."
"I have no idea why he/she is texting me."
"I am in the process of getting a divorce."
"I got tied up at the office."
"Money isn't important."
"My battery died."
"I had no phone signal."
"That was incredible sex."
"We're just friends."
"I was only kidding."
"I'm not married."
"I didn't sleep with her."

Actively repeating a lie or denial does not make it true.

However, if someone repeats a denial or lie often enough, there *are* those who will believe them. These are usually the people who *want* to believe them anyway. They are the people who love the liar and want to believe the best about them.

Evidence to the contrary will be seen as false, planted, contrived, or somehow otherwise excusable… in the liar's mind.

The grapevine still hums loudly with facts. We now not only *hear* it through the grapevine, we can *see* it and *read* all about it, too. We are simply left to decide if we want to choose to believe the serial liars or cope, while holding our heads high, or walk away.

> *"The more people rationalize cheating,*
> *the more it becomes a culture of dishonesty.*
> *And that can become a vicious, downward cycle.*
> *Because suddenly, if everyone else is cheating,*
> *you feel a need to cheat, too."*
>
> —Stephen Covey (1932 – 2012)
> American author

Tip: Respect yourself. Respect the facts.

35
The Sign Says

In 1977, Fleetwood Mac's "Rumours" album featured a Stevie Nicks song called, "Dreams." It warned us that no matter how special a player makes us feel when they focus on us, their love will be gone when they are done playing. Sadly, this plays out in real life if your lover happens to be a player.

Let's say that you and your husband have a regular social routine, such as a special night when you go out together each week to socialize with friends at a particular restaurant's Happy Hour.

Suddenly, he starts having excuses why you can't go. Perhaps he's working late, he has a meeting, he'll still be on the road, he "conveniently" gets home too late to go, one of his guy pals wants to talk with him alone, etc.

Then, after a time, you learn that he's been going to that very same Happy Hour *without* you and being quite the happy social beast. Oh, oh. No kidding. You are cramping his "style."

Quite simply, some people want it both ways. They want the security of your marriage or committed relationship AND the flexibility and freedom of single status. They want to come and go just as they did before you, and they do not want to be held accountable to anyone.

Oh, but they do expect *you* to hold fast to the commitment role, because that is important to them. Hmmm. This is obviously an immature thought process. *They* want to play, but they expect *you* to *not* play. Respect yourself enough to call cheaters out for the self-centered egotists they are.

Affairs and cheating can be physical or emotional… or both. Regardless, they are devastating to both the victim and the relationship they are destroying. Plus, they nix the cheater's chances of having *any* honest relationship, especially if they rationalize or try to justify their illicit behaviors.

One lovely woman experienced this and learned that her husband was actually trying to make people think that their marriage was on the rocks. He made up criticisms and pretended that they were fighting all the time. He'd even gone as far as to tell some people that they were divorcing.

Sure enough, he had been secretly dating someone… a woman from their weekly social night group. Oops. When his wife found out, she offered to make his divorce claims come true.

Studies show that the vast majority of cheaters are sexually satisfied at home. The missing connection tends to be an emotional one, and this is as true for men as for women.

It's usually *not* because they seek an exploit with someone younger or better looking. It's because they seek some emotional gratification that they are not getting at home.

Often someone gets the urge to cheat after one of their friends has admitted to cheating. Or, if a friend is going through a rough patch in a relationship, this can spur a rough patch in your own relationship. If a friend's marriage has just broken up, and you are living with someone with the cheating/ flirting/cavorting tendency, get ready for a rough ride.

When someone cheats on us, the door is opened to all sorts of mangled negative thinking. I'm not worthy; I'm unattractive; I'm not worthy; I'm not interesting any longer; I'm not "enough" for my spouse anymore; I'm not worthy. We lose our self-confidence and self-respect because of something someone *else* did! The cheater is fully responsible for his or her actions. Get it off **your** shoulders!

The sorry comedy of the matter is that when someone gets caught in one phase or another of "the hunt" or "the follow through," they tend to get *very* upset. Unfortunately, they are usually not upset that *they* have been found to not be the loyal and true partner they want to be or pretended to be. They're upset that they got *caught*.

Getting caught means they can't escape the fact that they really did hurt someone. It dispels their wacky thinking that their illicit behavior has no negative impact on the person they love. It's all ridiculous and truly pathetic garbage, but it's dished out every day.

My husband is a highly social beast. He loves going out, especially when there's live music. We do this together a lot. When he travels, he goes out alone.

I offered what our male friends call an extremely liberal policy. "Leave it at the bar."

In other words, socialize and enjoy yourself, but there should be no phone number exchanges or plans to meet again… unless it includes both of us. He should present himself as the happily married man he is and not pretend to be single or available. Even if someone is insisting he take their business card, simply say, "Thank you." At the end of the evening, however, slide it back to them, making it very clear that it is his *intention* to *not* take their information with him.

I certainly do not expect him to sit and watch TV all evening. But I do expect him to be respectful of me and us.

Some people say that mixed socializing can go too far, especially at a bar. My response to that is rather simplistic also. If you would not have any qualms whatsoever about what you are doing or what is being said if your spouse suddenly walked in and joined you, then it's unlikely you've crossed any line.

Still, too many people have no discipline. They like the ego boost of someone or several people showing interest in them. They simply can't back off, despite the fact that they are happily in a committed relationship.

If someone is NOT happy being in their relationship, then they should have the decency to end the relationship BEFORE they start flirting and playing the field.

Well, that's what *should* happen. That is rare however. Typically, someone simply cheats, sometimes again and again, without regard for who gets hurt. They are merely pleasing themselves.

Indicate THIS

In hindsight to a cheating situation, we often hear that there were signs, and many were clear. Yet, we didn't see it coming. We tend to put on blinders and believe what is said to us, despite what may be obvious. That is less painful than believing that someone we love and trust is not being loving, nor trustworthy.

Are or were there signs or indicators that something was amiss? We rarely find lipstick on a collar or sense an odd perfume. You might find things in the car such as odd gum wrappers or an empty coffee cup from a place you never go, but most cheaters are pretty quick to clean up such tell-tale evidence. You might find receipts for flowers or some intimate gift that you didn't receive, but cheaters in this high-tech world typically use cash or have hidden credit card accounts for these endeavors and discard all receipts.

Usually, the first thing that signals something is wrong is anything you might classify as a change in your beloved's behavior. Changes can occur in any number of arenas, and they often happen in more than one. The following is a partial list of cheating indicators when they appear as changes to the norm in your relationship.

Intimacy

Less or increased sexual or emotional interest
Avoidance of contact, both physical and intellectual
Distances himself from you emotionally
Stops confiding in you
Avoids being alone with you
Stops saying "I love you"
Resists holding your hand in public
Doesn't look you in the eye
Some new sexual taste… or even just a different style of kissing

Displays a new "talent" during sex
Suddenly wants to try something exotic with you
Has a new interest in pornography
Shows reluctance to kiss you
Increasingly has excuses to not make love with you

Attitude Towards You

Moody around you lately
Nervous laughter
Fidgety or irritable about doing something with you
Highly defensive to questions about whereabouts or behaviors
Critical of things you do that never bothered him previously
Brings up the way you look or the weight you've gained
Suddenly compliments you excessively
You just can't do anything right in their eyes any more
Acts aloof towards you
Shifts from being happy to being distant when someone walks in
Suddenly encourages you to go out of town to visit family and such

Conversation

Picks fights with you
Tries to argue about anything for an excuse to storm out
Accuses you of having an affair
Change in the pitch or pacing of conversation with you
Stops asking for your advice or opinion
Highly defensive or emotional if you bring up your suspicion
Starts speaking to you with disrespect and sarcasm
Uses prefaces to statements such as "You won't believe this, but…"
Stops listening to you
Starts charging you with not doing your share around the house
Claims to just be stressed from work

Technology

Changes the computer screen when you enter the room
Sets up a new email account and keeps it secret from you
Stops adding names for caller IDs to phone numbers
Starts deleting emails and text messages

Walks outside or to another room to take certain phone calls
Starts demanding you not touch their phone, never mind answer it
A new number or numbers start showing up on your bill… a lot
Starts regularly deleting the call records on their cell phone
Claims to miss your calls because of no cell service for several hours
Suddenly not available to take your calls at work
Purchases a second cell phone and doesn't tell you
Hides the second phone's bill or pays/prepays it online
Doesn't respond promptly to your voicemail or text messages
Turns phone off during times he used to be easily accessible
Suggests you not call as he'll be at a work conference all weekend
More ATM withdrawals appear on your accounts
Password protects computer and doesn't give you the password
Starts spending lots of time on the computer, especially with email
Spends lots of time on the Internet, especially late nights
Erases browser history immediately
Excessive car mileage though they insist they only went to the office

Behavior

Stays away from home more; doesn't seem to be around any more
Lots of excuses for absences
Seems very forgetful or distracted at home
Stops wearing wedding ring… for very "logical" reasons
Heads straight to the shower when arrives home
Dresses differently for work than used to dress
Gives you flowers or gifts for no reason
Sudden devotion to working out at the gym
Starts sleeping on the sofa at least part of the night
Suddenly likes a different music that they did not like previously
Has a new affection for a comedian you have never heard together
Doesn't tell you where he's going or where he's been
Goes out to run a simple errand and returns hours later
Buys new clothes, but doesn't wear them in front of you
Hesitates to be seen with you in public
Seems to go to more "no spouses" events for work
Suddenly becomes a flirt
Starts paying great attention to appearance, even to run errands
Talks about new bars and clubs, but won't ever take you there

Body Language
Angles away from you when you talk
Shrugs shoulders when making a statement or claim
Changes facial expression in front of some other woman/man
When out at a bar, sits angled away from you

Personal
Changes in style of dress, or colors worn
Takes time off from work, when you think they are at work
Always has an excuse prepared when arriving home late
Tries a new hairstyle
Wears a new cologne
Has unexplained scratches or bruises
He starts man-scaping, or she suddenly gets a Brazilian

Intuition
You feel it in your gut that something is wrong
Instinct tells you something is off with your mate
You sense their behavior just does not add up

Observation
A new person is on the scene… "just a friend" or "new coworker"
Returns home with a different fragrance than when they left
Enthusiasm over a new person, especially if it's highly critical
Brings up a particular person repeatedly… to throw you off track
Goes on more business trips, but has excuses for you to stay home
You find condoms or birth control pills
Your friends or social circle start acting strangely toward you
Claims lots of overtime, but it never shows up on the pay check
Spouse's coworkers suddenly act aloof toward you
There's suddenly less money… a lot less money… in the budget

Important Points

Even when a cheater gets caught cheating, they rarely confess. They will continue to deny, despite the evidence. Or they will twist it to make it seem as if it was your fault or your jealousy or your vivid imagination.

Ignore them. Cheaters lie. Hello! When they get caught, they lie more.

When a cheater cheats on you, it's actually *not* about *you*.

They may surely have started telling friends and co-workers that you are a shrew or won't have sex with them or whatever they want to say. They may have started totally bitching you out and trying to pick fights… to justify their cheating.

When I was divorcing a cheating, now EX-husband, he threatened to "tell everyone" that I was frigid and wouldn't have sex with him. I told him to go right ahead.

Any bogus excuse will do.

We've all heard the malarkey that ranges from men aren't supposed to be monogamous to there being a gene that predisposes a man to cheat. All bogus.

Societies that have condoned male cheating and condemned female cheating are simply male-dominated cultures. Cheating is cheating, no matter who is doing it. It's wrong.

Cheating reveals an individual who is insecure, egotistical, or lacking in self-discipline. Anyone can cheat.

It takes commitment and character to stay true to your partner.

That said, if you don't fear your spouse may be cheating on you, don't now get obsessed with looking for changes in behaviors. Just because it seems that cheating is on the rise does *not* mean that *your* relationship has become infected. It doesn't work that way.

If your sex life is delightful, good. If your conversation is still as lively and intimate as ever, good. If you are still going places together and having fun together, good. If you both dress for each other, share with each other, and focus on each other's needs, good.

To further "affair-proof" a relationship, we should be very open with each other. That means that we talk about things that might otherwise not get discussed.

For example, you and your partner have agreed to a committed relationship with each other. Talk about what being monogamous specifically means to you… and to your spouse.

We need an understanding of how we feel ourselves AND how *they* feel. Then we can both make and maintain a full commitment. There's no gray area. You've talked about it.

Try dating each other… do LOTS of fun things together. Leave no time to cheat.

Again, keep a good sense of humor. For example, my husband's heart throb for years has been the actress Jennifer Aniston. If she ever shows up, The Ronald gets a "hall pass."

Remember, no relationship is perfect. There will always be ups and downs. There will be ebbs and flows of passion and happiness.

Tip: Do have fun together. Unless you are dealing with a complete narcissist, this diminishes the chances that there would be any interest in straying.

36
Snoop Dog

*"Never expect loyalty
from a person that can't give you honesty."*
-- Surgeo Bell
American Life Coach

Wouldn't it be nice to be in a relationship where both parties can actually trust each other? Some have this blessing; others do not.

While I always say we should never take our loved ones for granted, I actually believe that we *should* be able to count on their loyalty, without a doubt. But what does a person do when their beloved lacks the discipline or inner strength to *actually* be the loyal, trustworthy person they *want* to be?

There are plenty of electronic snooping technologies available these days. The best are those that two people agree on to let each other know their location and safety.

They can easily see other slices of the "paper trail" pie. For example, phone bill details and credit card statements should never be considered "off limits" to each other. If someone is hiding some credit card's bills or existence, they often are doing this so their partner won't know how much they are going out, shopping, etc.

In a strong relationship, such thinking is thankfully unnecessary. However, when one person in a relationship is not behaving properly, this couple is apt to eventually or suddenly split up.

Trust in loyalty is one of the absolute most essential elements.

Once broken, the offender only compounds their problem when they yell at the victim or try to transfer their issues to them. "Well, I never would have done that if you weren't so ____." Fill in the blank with anything. Any excuse will do when a perpetrator is trying to deflect attention away from their own crimes.

"Never cheat on someone who is good to you. Karma is a bitch."

-- Surgeo Bell
American Life Coach

Paul had learned that Jane was flirting with a couple of other men. His wife denied it vehemently. He knew she'd been behaving more secretively than usual, but he hadn't given a thought to the fact that she might be going out on him.

When the phone bill arrived, he went to the detail section for her cell phone and saw two unfamiliar numbers that had several calls, both incoming and outgoing. When Paul had told her what he'd heard, Jane's angry overreaction had made him suspicious. Now he found himself using online sources to learn who owned the new numbers that appeared on their bill.

Sure enough, they belonged to men with whom they'd had no prior dealings. One she'd met through work, and the other she'd been seeing frequently at their regular pub.

"No wonder Jane was always going there at least an hour before me," Paul said. "I thought she was developing a drinking problem. Now I know it's a cheating problem."

Paul got out of work early one afternoon so he could arrive unannounced and two hours early one evening. Sure enough, there was Jane, sitting side-by-side with a man named Bob. Their heads were together and they were giggling and chatting and sharing an appetizer.

They didn't see him come in, so he just walked up and sat down beside her. Jane gave a casual glance his way and almost fell of her bar stool. The shock on her face was crystal clear.

While her husband introduced himself to her "friend," she stammered and stuttered foolishly. Bob was not impressed to find that his new gal pal had fabricated her entire scenario. Plus, she had been brazen enough to regularly meet with him at the same restaurant she frequented with her husband, who, it turned out, arrived regularly just 30 minutes after Bob always left for work.

Jane had told him that she and Paul were getting a divorce because he was abusive, lazy, and a cheater. She lied. What a surprise.

Bob had felt like her prince, rescuing her. Now he felt like her palace jester. All he could do was apologize to Paul, assuring him that he would never have gotten involved with Jane if he'd had a clue that she was lying. He'd had it done to him in the past, and his remorse was genuine.

Paul told him not to worry and added that they'd probably have become good friends, had they met under different circumstances.

Then Paul's attention turned to Jane. If she thought their marriage was going to continue, she needed to come clean. She also needed counseling. He'd go, too, but this was non-negotiable. Plus, certain behaviors had to change immediately, because she had a long way back to earn his trust.

Obviously, one change was that she should not go out to any bar without him. She'd blown his trust. Period. He also suggested she get a part-time job, not because they needed the money, but because she needed something positive to do with her afternoons.

Jane was very fortunate to have Paul's love and understanding. He stood by her side while she and the counselor figured out her issues and started to deal with them.

The Bimbo Has Brains

Their marriage has become strong and healthy. They both ended up glad that Paul had snooped. He saw warning signs and was able to nip the problem in the bud, so to speak.

> *"You didn't just cheat on me; you cheated on us.*
> *You didn't just break my heart; you broke our future."*
> —Steve Maraboli (1975 -)
> American commentator and author

Often, relationship manipulations and untrustworthy behavior continue for years. Eventually, the unwitting spouse will find out beyond a shadow of a doubt, and push often comes to shove.

* * * * * * * * * * *

Sherry was totally distraught. She'd reached for his sunglass case in his car side pocket and came up with a "burner" phone instead. She felt her whole body start to tremble. Sherry pulled Stan's car off the road. She just sat there for a few moments, with thoughts racing from abandonment to wondering why she'd ever driven his car for that errand. Denial would not take it away.

She looked at the phone. It was a type they'd never owned. She powered it up. Fifty minutes of call records and all text messages had been deleted. Hoping desperately that this was some mistake or someone else's lost phone, she opened the phone info setting and saw the phone owner's name. One word confirmed her fears…
Stan.

Then Sherry opened the Contacts folder and saw half a dozen ladies' names and numbers, primarily from the Austin, Texas area, less than one hour from where they were trying to sell their former house.

She resisted the temptation to dial one of the numbers and introduce herself. No need. She knew none of them would have a clue that Stan was married.

Her mind raced. Now she "got" why he had been getting nastier and nastier with her lately. She had been giving him the benefit of the doubt, recognizing he was dealing with back pain and their financial struggles.

They'd been trying to sell their old home in San Marcos, Texas for over 4 years. Upgrades and changes just seemed to create a money pit to which there was no end. Still, not a single offer had come out of the showings.

While they lived in their new home in Nashville, Tennessee, nearly 900 miles away, they'd traveled back to San Marcos numerous times to maintain the property, plus add a couple extensions, creating a gorgeous gourmet chef's kitchen and a new, enlarged en suite for the master bedroom wing. They'd designed everything themselves, and it was beautiful.

At one point three years earlier, when he needed to be there for three weeks, he'd taken a couple of his male construction acquaintances with him to Texas to help on some work, but he'd had Sherry stay in Nashville. Later she'd learned that Stan had met a woman in an Austin piano bar one night and had literally been regularly dating her ever since.

That woman had no clue that he was even married. On the second or third time they'd gone out to dinner, she'd asked him that question point blank, and Stan had told her that he'd been divorced for more than 10 years.

Following this affair coming to light, Stan had initially said the other woman was lying and that he didn't even know her. He then tried to say that he recalled one of the construction guys being interested in some woman. Finally, he came clean, apologized, and swore it would never happen again.

Sherry felt sick. She *now* believed that all he meant was that he would never get *caught* again.

To give her more confidence as he was now traveling there more often alone, he'd added a security camera in the San Marcos house. That would let Sherry look in whenever she wanted to feel more secure when he traveled there.

He had said that money was the reason she couldn't go with him. She fully cooperated with his requests to not spend money unnecessarily. He, too, would feed himself from the wide variety of food and meals that they'd stocked in the San Marcos freezer. Well, that never quite worked out.

"Big deal," Sherry thought. "He's never home for me to see him on camera anyway. The camera just meant he wouldn't bring a woman home again…. without first disconnecting the camera."

Every time that Stan had to go to San Marcos, Texas, whether it was for a few days or a week, he did not stay home even one single evening. He was frequenting his favorite bars in San Marcos and finding some new ones in Austin.

Stan was burning the midnight oil the entire time. Once he'd get home, he'd complain bitterly about how exhausted he was from all the work he'd done.

One evening, when she'd called him while he was out at a bar, Sherry said she'd calmly suggested that he try staying home once in a while. He'd started yelling at her that she had no idea how stressful doing all this work really was. "How dare you, after all the crap I'm going through!"

Now her head was spinning. He was acting all self-righteous. In truth, he'd been out there on the Austin social scene behaving as if he was single, available, and interested in other women.

He'd even pretended to be home on several nights when he'd actually gone out. Stan told her that he was watching TV in the bedroom, but the security system told the real story… over and over again.

He'd go out as early as 4pm and stay out till at least 10 or 10:30 and sometimes till well after midnight. Stan seemed helpless when it came to bands, bars, and babes… though not necessarily in that order.

Sherry was not an angry person. When she regained her composure after finding the "burner" phone, however, she knew this was the final betrayal. On this very same day she'd initiated a quiet conversation to see if he might be ready for them to go their separate ways.

He'd exuded such anger toward her lately. There seemed to be nothing she could do right when it came to him.

Stan had looked stunned. Not only did he swear his love to her, but he'd added that he'd marry her again in a blink. No, in half a blink. They were forever together, and he couldn't be happier.

But Sherry saw "forever" coming to an end. She could no longer tolerate living with someone she could not trust.

She recalled a rare trip with him to San Marcos about a month earlier. One night when they'd finished working early in the afternoon, she'd tried to get Stan to take her out to one of the new clubs he'd found in Austin.

He'd mistakenly pulled out a coupon from a hip Austin restaurant, so she'd learned about the sassy 6th Street neighborhood that had become such a draw to him. But Stan had moaned and groaned about Austin being too far a drive.

In truth it was just half an hour away from their house, and they had gone there for various events in the past. It seemed that he now had a powerful need to keep her away from Austin in the evening.

Sherry's suspicion had been piqued. Now the "burner" phone confirmed her fears.

Stan was behaving like an out-of-control child. He wanted the marriage and Sherry, but he also wanted to act unmarried whenever he wanted. Well, that pattern is certainly not something he invented.

Sherry said the party was over. If he could not acknowledge that he had problems… some *serious* problems… she could no long enable the craziness. It broke her heart, but this was simply too hurtful and stressful. She knew she did not deserve to be treated this sourly. But Stan was struggling to accept that he was in need of professional help.

Sometimes very nice people have to deal with some far-from-nice pieces of reality in relationships. When signals ring clearly that something is amiss, follow your instincts. You may be able to uncover the truth and work together to piece your relationship back together.

It's amazing how many cheaters and liars believe they won't be caught. *News Flash*: In today's age of technology, there won't just be a paper trail. There will be multiple electronic and digital trails, as well.

Tip: You may have to let a relationship end in order to regain sanity and health in your own life.

241

Section 10
LIGHTEN UP

37
Unconditional Love

*Every day you may want to relive your life
and do some things over,
but it's not every day you can find with whom.*

My parents live in a wonderful independent living facility. It's one of those that enables seniors to transition seamlessly to assisted living, rehabilitation, nursing care, and even hospice. Their numerous friendships there form the most wonderful support system.

I couldn't help but marvel at one beautiful couple... a true example of unconditional love. She had moved into the Alzheimer's unit, and no longer recognized her husband of more than 50 years. He bought a home just a block away, so he could visit her more easily. And visit he does... every single day. He pushes her wheelchair into the enclosed garden and sits beside her on a bench. He lovingly brushes her hair and talks to her for several hours.

Each day she believes she meets him for the first time. She always asks the nurse to tell her his name after he goes home and comments on what a nice man he is. The next day, she meets him all over again... for the first time. He does not have to visit. She would not miss him if he missed a day. But he comes. And he shares lovingly with her. Then he goes home.

That is unconditional love. He loves her, not for anything she can do for him. He gives and gives and gives, with no expectation of anything in return. And yet, she gives all that she has, too.

*Any home can be a castle
when the King and Queen are in love.*

Unconditional love is with you no matter what you do or don't do. We often think of it with regard to how a parent feels about their new baby. We hear it in church with regard to God's unconditional love for Jesus.

And yet, couples can also enjoy this pure love, although it is definitely not where relationships begin.

Unconditional love takes a strong and deliberate evolution.

Unconditional love is not the "love is blind" syndrome. It's not blind to a partner's faults or vulnerabilities. Rather, it accepts the entire package, pros and cons. They can see our very worst, and they still love us.

No decision is needed when we become romantically involved with someone. However, if we want unconditional love for that loving relationship, we *must* make a decision. In fact, we probably need to start each day with that same decision. We will love without expecting the person receiving it to do or give a thing.

Unconditional love is way beyond emotional involvement. This is loving the person inside the person… loving their very soul.

It may not be possible for everyone, but it is fun to at least try. Remember, it's not emotional. It requires action… daily. Often we learn to love unconditionally by showing love to people who are not being very loving, never mind likeable.

It could be the aggressive driver who is hogging the road that you simply let slide into the line of traffic in front of you. Perhaps it's someone entering a building, and you open the door for them. Maybe you pay for someone else's cup of coffee… someone you don't even know or ever expect to meet.

Practicing giving love with no expectations of anything in return helps us in our most important personal relationship with another person. Some argue that a spouse will use you if you show unconditional love. I disagree most heartily.

Loving someone unconditionally does not mean letting your partner walk all over you. Set boundaries.

Leave if need be. End the relationship if it is too painful. That does not mean that you did not love unconditionally. Quite the opposite. If you love and serve and give without expectation of the same positive love in return, you are loving unconditionally. If your partner cheats or lies or hits you, you do *not* have to stay.

The person we love may not encourage our passions. They may squelch our creativity. They may try to hold us back. We give unconditional love without expecting our needs to be met in return. That doesn't mean that at some point we won't decide that we've had enough of that relationship. It's okay to move on in life. You can still love that person unconditionally, though you can no longer live with them.

This is not contradictory to the idea of loving without expecting anything in return. However, while you do not have an expectation of them loving you back as you wish you could be loved, this does not mean you don't deserve respect and basic decency.

Where people enjoy mutual unconditional love, you will also find mutual respect. Mutual unconditional love is a very rare situation indeed. Just imagine the beauty and happiness when two people give unconditional love to each other. Still, we need to remember that loving unconditionally does not guarantee you will also be loved back, never mind be given unconditional love. That is okay.

Your partner may or may not be able to evolve into a person who can give unconditional love. That has no bearing on *your* ability to give *them* unconditional love. Setting the consistent example can help them learn to give unconditional love, too. This is a conscious, daily decision and involves action, remember.

With unconditional love, people recognize that no one can make you feel happy. That must come from inside of each of us.

No one can make you feel angry. That must come from inside of each of us. No one can be in a relationship with the expectation of being fulfilled by someone else.

Unconditional Love

It is far from easy to learn to not project our wishes on someone else. It's part of human nature. We want to feel loved by the person we love. We want to feel acceptance and value.

However, loving unconditionally means giving, with no expectation of getting. One of the things we must give is true, genuine forgiveness. That includes forgiving ourselves for all our own trespasses and weaknesses.

Worry less about the people in the world who spread hate by killing innocent people. They think they have a purpose and are making a point. They are misguided at best, deranged at worst. We do not change a culture "en masse" or by force. In truth, martyring innocent people under the guise of promoting a "cause" turns people away from that cause. We best change a culture and ways of thinking one person at a time and by showing positive gains.

We must understand that disappointment, rejection, and pain are part of life. They need not control us or our ability to love unconditionally, though the negative feelings in life will always be around. People will still hurt us and people we love. We can still get our heart broken. We can't earn someone else's love; we can merely give love.

Regardless, whoever we are, we can make a positive difference in someone's life every single day. That is a worthy goal. We will literally feel great pleasure just in living a life that offers service to someone daily.

We must start the journey to unconditional love with self-acceptance. None of us is perfect, but when we can accept ourselves as we are, we can also accept someone else. When we can love ourselves, we can love someone else. We can try to improve or change things about ourselves, but we know *not* to try to change other people. We accept them.

My sister exemplifies unconditional love better than anyone I have ever known. With all our foibles, faux pas, and faults, she simply loves. Deborah has never been judgmental… just kind and giving.

She lives to serve. She loves everyone unconditionally. She lives by the saying, "Om shanti." This simply means, "I am a peaceful soul." And she is.

I remember once a number of years ago when Deborah asked to come visit me one night. We made nachos and chatted and laughed. Then she got down to the business of why she wanted to talk. She had memories of treating me as her servant when we were children, always having me get her this or that, waiting on her, and letting me take the blame for trouble she had caused.

I told her to let the guilt go. I was fine and not wounded by the experience in the slightest. Then, because of the wise cracker that I am, I threw in a memory of one thing that I had really disliked. Though just three years my senior, she had enjoyed calling me a baby at every opportunity.

"Oh, no-o-o-o," Deborah groaned. "You remember!"

I laughed and reminded her how she'd told me that when I turned four I would no longer be a baby. Riiiiight. When I turned four, she'd reconfigured it to calling me a "baby-type." Arrrgh!   I got her laughing at our childhood silliness. I guaranteed her that the mysterious head jerk and shoulder tick I was now displaying for her humor was surely only temporary. We laughed some more.

In her heart, Deborah ached for each and every wound she had ever caused anyone. I truthfully assured her that I had always viewed her as a most gentle, healing soul… even to a fault perhaps. To me, she is the closest thing to an angel living on this earth that I have ever known.

I say that again because, from my perspective, Deborah is a living example of unconditional love. It is quite simply the way she lives her life… every day. With patient work and daily disciplined actions, we can all love unconditionally. We can experience peace within our souls. We can live happily, expecting nothing in return.

Tip: Become free… with no strings attached.

38
<u>Affirmations</u>

The most important stakeholder in your life is you.

I have long been a believer in claiming the positive. This means focusing on what is good, the positive direction in which we are heading. Too many people "major on the minors," letting whatever is negative interfere with the rest of life… and the loved ones around them.

I'll say it again. No one wants to be around a person who can dull the shine on a brand new copper penny. Still, we all seem to know someone who brightens up a room simply by *leaving* it. That quip is light-hearted, but sadly true.

Why *not* choose to see the glass as half full, rather than half empty? See the day as mostly sunny, rather than partly cloudy. If there's a 30% chance of showers, then there's a 70% probability of NO showers. Even when life seems to have dealt us a bad hand, there must be things we can celebrate. They may seem to be the tiniest items to us at some point in time, but they can add up to a wonderful life… if we let them.

To start and end each day on the right note, I like to remind myself of even just a few things for which I am grateful. I have my health. I have two living parents… and my Mom's twin sister, who I literally call my Other Mother. I live in a warm home. I am loved by a wonderful man. I have an awesome brother, sister, step-children, niece and nephews, and extended families.

Make a list. Write down every little thing you can think of, and you'll likely have a very long list. It matters little to anyone else what your affirmations are. It matters greatly to you that you know your list. They can be a simple as, "I have a nice smile." They can be as grand as, "I am steadily focused on my goals for financial independence." Perhaps you are grateful to have a good job or wonderful co-workers. We should always express appreciation for good health, a roof over our heads, and great friends.

If we have a loving spouse, healthy children, or other living family members, we have an abundance of wealth for which to be grateful. We can give thanks for strong faith and a close, personal relationship with God. We can appreciate the beauty of nature around us. We can be grateful for whatever our specific talents might be, from sports, dancing, or cooking, to growing flowers, solving math problems, or doing crossword puzzles.

Many years ago, while still just a college student, I started writing down long lists of things for which I was grateful, nuances and interests that made me who I was. Things that made me happy. Whether I had those things or not mattered little.

Many people advocate that these lists need to be affirmations of what you are doing "right" to reach your goals. For example, "I am saving 20% of my income each week." Or, "My self-esteem improves daily." Or, "I look forward to greeting each new day."

This approach works. This is claiming the positive to encourage ourselves to think better of ourselves and what we are doing. However, there are other positive lists that I found most helpful for me. Following a heartbreaking end to an early relationship, I found myself particularly "down" on myself. I felt worthless, sad, and misunderstood.

The list I wrote healed my aching heart and soul, because it reminded me of many of the things I liked about me. My worth was not reliant on someone else's love for me.

I turned my list into a long, skinny poster that I kept ever since. All these decades later, the list would be far longer. Still, I share my original list with you now to illustrate how basic and simplistic items on such an accounting can be, and yet still be highly effective.

Though at the time I wrote it, I did not feel as hopeful as I may have wanted, the exercise helped me to remember the many things that made me happy or inspired me. Things that gave me peace or made me smile. Places I wanted to go or liked going, and things I wanted to do or enjoyed doing.

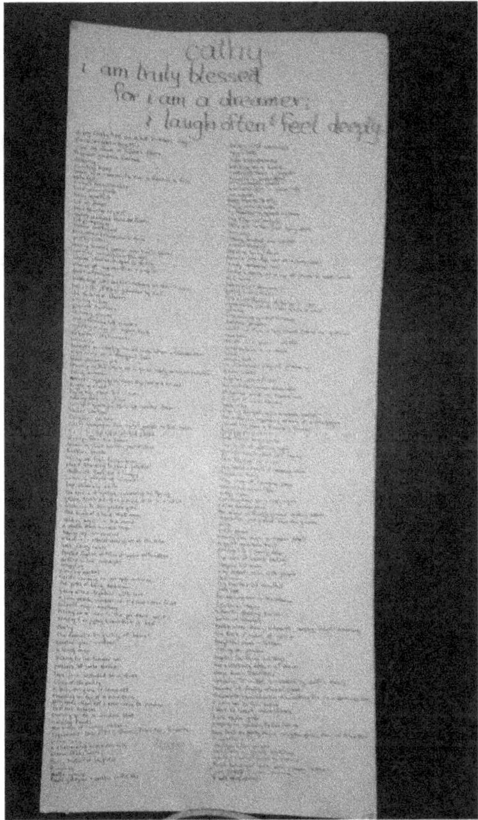

I titled it simply, "Cathy… I am truly blessed, for I am a dreamer; I laugh often and feel deeply." I followed that with my list in two columns of phrases and words.

A big shady tree on a hot summer day
Candlelight – any time
Rippling waves at a lake's shore
Fragrant gardenia blossoms
Dreaming
Climbing trees
Steak, wine, and popcorn for two in
    front of a fire
Waterfalls
A man's touchable shirt
Lush, green plants
Being barefoot
Lit oil lamps
Time to write or paint
Cooking someone's favorite foods

Old photographs
Shared excitement
Back roads between small towns
Pretty clothes
Making someone special know they're
    special
Summer raindrops on the roof
Lobster chunks dipped in butter
Stories of long ago times and people
Quiet afternoons
Little boys who see their fathers as their
heroes
The cliffs of Maui pounded by surf
Old-fashioned blouses
Sterling silver

Peacock feathers
Watching clouds
Long, relaxing hot showers
Reading a play or a good book
Fabulous restaurants
Unicorns
Sunlight on a freshly mowed lawn after
a thunderstorm
A log cabin on a tranquil lake
Standing on the stage of a quiet, nearly
darkened theatre
Fresh blueberry pie
Being a woman
Nature's ingenuity in never duplicating
a sunset
Anything suede
Flying high above the clouds
Making love – anytime
Sunlight sparkling through ice-coated
trees
Broiled seafood
European castles
Sipping champagne from crystal goblets
on the beach
The first crisp apple of the season
Singing from the heart
Dreaming about endless possibilities
Babbling brooks
Skiing on fresh fallen snow
People stretching to reach potential
Heathcliff, Garfield, and Snoopy
Watching people at airports
Long, leisurely walks
The smells of Nature awakening in
spring
Getting drunk-out-of-my-mind once in a
while
Listening to the garden grow
The touch of a hand that cares
Making angels in the snow
A choice steak now and then
Having my hair brushed
A bonfire in a forest clearing or at the
shore
Soft, flowy skirts
Toasted English muffins dripping with
butter
Driving in the moonlight

Snuggling
Planning parties
Horses running in an open meadow
The pride of being American
Being alone together with love
Juicy peach, cranberries, cold citrus
Colored magic markers
Fishing on a lake in the pre-dawn mist
Serving and enjoying breakfast in bed
Poetry
The dramatic tranquility of sunset
Beveled glass windows
A loving man
Basking in the summer sun
Platters of jumbo shrimp
Love in a secluded sand dune
Lilies of the valley
A tall, cool glass of lemonade
Standing on top of a mountain
Spicy foods, from hot 'n sour soup to
nachos
Summer breezes
Curling up on a window seat
Holding hands
The flavor of country western
Jaguar XJS, Porsche 944, Camaro,
Trans Am, Corvette
Warm toes
A challenging character role
Warm, flaky pastry
Full, contented laughter
Fireworks
Subtle incense
Friendly dragons and castles in the sky
Crispy, cold mornings
Hay rides
Ripe strawberries
Walking on a beach
Cuddly kittens and puppies
Browsing in bookstores
Soft, buckskin jackets
A secluded glen in springtime
Old movies
Being free to be silly
Fresh piña coladas
My footsteps' icy squeak on snow
The flight of seagulls
Little girls in their first fancy dress

Affirmations

Hot dogs
Feeling needed and wanted
Window shopping
The wind on my face
Sunrise over the mist of a rocky coast
A busy rehearsal hall
Holding a toasty warm cup of cocoa in
  both hands
Full moon
Candlelight dinners
Grassy hills and fields
The alive feeling of being in love
Aquamarine, white, plum, black,
  and rose
Purring
Entertaining special friends
Scented candles
Shuffling thru crispy fall maple leaves
Rainbows
Velvet, silk, satin, and chiffon
Wind chimes and crickets
Lilacs
Driving fast
An occasional day of pampering
Koala bears
Tropical paradises
An old-fashioned clambake
Whispered words of tenderness
A field of wildflowers
Backrubs
Sharing thoughts with someone special
The undeniably appealing aroma of a
  barbeque
Wandering through a friendly forest
Building sandcastles
Food-filled magazines
The thrill of opening night
Quaint New England port towns
The "feeling" of music
The sound and smell of popping corn
Flowering trees
Long, languid, lounging days
Being alone now and then
Sleigh rides
Counting stars on a clear night

Making someone smile
The aroma of freshly ground coffee
  beans
Vegetables, just picked from the garden
Morning dew drops on
  flower petals
A quiet mountain trail
Dancing till I nearly drop
The smell of bread baking
Sleeping till noon
City streets alive with people
Red roses
The season's first snowfall
Junk food
Morning sun in the kitchen
Christmas trees
A tearful standing ovation
Barbequed chicken
Good movies – funny, dramatic,
  moving, thought-provoking
The first flowers of spring
Thoughtful cards and letters
Sitting on porches
Tropical Caribbean holidays
The revitalizing effect of dawn
Deep, fresh snowfalls
Watching TV in bed, surrounded by
  edible treats
Mounds of freshly whipped cream
The warmth and special privacy of a
  crackling fire in a darkened room
A carnival in full swing
Heart to heart conversations
Fresh maple syrup
Jumping in crunchy fallen leaves
Bare feet on plushy carpet, rich green
  grass, fur, or fine sand
Thoughtful gifts
Cartoons and comedies
Being totally quiet, sometimes
Needing and being needed by someone
Fresh, hot bread with soft, creamy butter
Just-picked flowers, anytime
A soft sand dollar

Okay, I admit it. I got more than a little carried away. However, what interested me in re-reading my old poster is that I cannot remember the hurt feelings from the young man with whom I'd suffered the heartache. By focusing on things that pleased me, or inspired me, I'd made a list that let me connect with myself. That is very healing in itself.

Sometimes, especially in times of pain, it can be difficult to see value in ourselves. So, let your list reflect things you appreciate around you. It's a great exercise in self-awareness.

Perhaps you can smile for friends with strong talents. You can appreciate the beauty of a glorious sunrise or sunset. You can be humbled by the simple, easy love of a dog or cat. You might be able to look at a flower, and revel in its color or delicacy. You may dream of a trip to someplace special.

Tip: Making your list is personal and fulfilling. It delivers peace. It's affirming.

39
Genuine Forgiveness

The person we love could be abusive. They may be dealing drugs.
They may be cheating in business. They may have committed a
crime and be heading to prison.

This all may sound extreme, but it sets the stage for us to learn how
to love the sinner, though we hate the sin. A person we love can be
nasty and mean. They may hurt and disappoint us repeatedly. We
can still love them. We can forgive them.

Forgiving does not mean forgetting. Trust has been shattered.
Hearts have been broken. Someone has behaved very badly. All
these things are impossible to forget. We are forever changed by
misdeeds done against us. However, we can forgive.

Forgiveness must start with learning to forgive ourselves. None of
us is perfect, and we have done our share of hurtful behaviors and
said our share of evil words. We cannot go back and change our
past. We can learn not to do these things in the future.

For someone carrying a great deal of personal baggage from their
past, this can be a daunting task. When a person has acted selfishly
and hurt people in the process, forgiving oneself and moving on is
an enormous challenge. If we continue trying to live *down* our past
actions, it's more difficult to live *up* to being the loving person we
want to be.

When we are the party that has been wronged, we often feel
obligated to forgive, even if our partner hasn't asked for it. This
becomes even tougher when the offender holds out and doesn't
acknowledge the pain they've caused by lies, abuse, cheating, or
even an affair.

Genuine forgiveness really deserves a genuine apology, not just for
hurting the loved one, but to express our understanding that we are
fully responsible for our error in judgment, words, and action.

Otherwise, how can a partner not believe there is a good chance they will be hurt again… and again… in the same manner?

Apologies require taking *full* responsibility. No half-truths, no partial admissions, no rationalizations, no finger pointing, and no justifications belong in any apology.

Why did I do this awful thing? I could be self-centered. I could be thoughtless. I could be insecure. My partner may NOT have been letting me down at all. In fact, my partner may not have even been failing to meet a deep need of mine. I may be clinging to those pesky unresolved past issues and was too weak or in too much denial to get help with my own baggage. Otherwise, I would avoid dumping my baggage on them.

In a genuine apology, I should explain why I *won't* cross that line again… why I beg their forgiveness… and how I will work to rebuild their trust in me… the trust that I shattered.

"They" say that women forgive, but don't forget, and men forget, but don't forgive. In my experience, that may seem true on the surface, but some men and women may *say* they've "talked it out" with the person they felt had offended them. They add that they've forgiven them and let it go.

However, the injustice, be it perceived or actual, lived just under the surface forevermore. This sore almost takes on a life of its own at any moment and without any recognizable provocation.

One man I know brought up an affronting conversation that had hurt him so deeply that I thought it had happened just two days before, not nearly two decades earlier.

Don't let wounds fester. Even silent resentment will hold you back and keep you in bondage to the anger and pain. Learn to forgive and set yourself free.

If you are spiritual, turn it over to God. We humans are weak and filled with flaws. Draw strength from your faith.

I always love it when people say, "Don't go to bed angry." Well, that doesn't mean that you and your partner must sit up all night if you are struggling to resolve a conflict. It can simply mean that you are releasing the anger and focusing on positives.

Imagine the positive resolution that you will reach with time. Focus on peaceful, uplifting images. Remember all the good and wonderful things that you truly are, despite any nastiness that may have been being spewed at you by the person who claims to love you. Think of things for which you are grateful. This is like programming yourself for restful sleep.

Guys are commonly known for arguing viciously with each other and then sharing a beer 30 minutes later. Typically, women need to fully understand *why* a friend hurt us. We usually need to talk it out and maybe have a good cry together before we can move past it.

Regardless, we all need and deserve genuine apologies, delivered with sincerity. Superficiality and casually laughing it off will just not fly. Know each other's boundaries and respect them. Talk about the boundaries. Make no assumptions that you both share the same ones. Stay in the present. Don't live in the past. Let all the wrongs stay in the past. Cease hostilities!

Whether someone has done something wrong or been wronged, their feelings are never wrong. If they are sad or angry or hurt or rejected, they have a right to feel that way. This does not mean that *we* are responsible for *their* feelings, any more than *they* are responsible for how *we* feel. When someone hurts us, and they will, *we* decide how to react or respond.

Believe in yourself and your thoughts so that no one can rattle you. No matter how loudly someone tries to berate you or put you down, remain calm. No matter how deftly someone may try to undermine your goals and dreams, stay at peace within yourself.

If an offender lives in total denial of their bad behavior and has no sincere desire to change, you can still forgive them, but you may also need to distance yourself from them.

This is sad, but sometimes true. We do not need to give negative, hurtful people the power to wound us repeatedly.

If we must leave someone we love, we do best when we can start fresh with forgiveness in our hearts. There's a 1946 French song. Albert Beach wrote English words in 1955. A number of artists have since recorded it. I particularly recall a Count Basie and Frank Sinatra rendition of, "I Wish You Love."

Though the singer's heart is breaking, the lyrics wish all good things to the parting lover, from sweet signs of spring to good health. They sing of setting the lover free with absolutely no hard feelings… just truly all the best wishes. To me, it sings of genuine forgiveness.

Seriously, how many of us have such positive wishes when a relationship ends with heartbreak? This is forgiveness for any and all pain and exudes unconditional love. The two do seem to go hand in hand.

Let all resentment go. Let all ill-will slide away. Let the ego stay at rest. We will remember the hurt, the injustice, and the trauma, but we can forgive the sinner.

Tip:

> *"There are two ways of spreading light.*
> *Be the candle or the mirror that reflects it."*
> -- Edith Wharton (1862-1937)
> American author

40
<u>Life is Funny That Way</u>

By this point, you know that I love quips and quotes. Throughout the project, whenever I know who said them or wrote them, I have given credit. Others are simply expressions that we hear now and then, in one configuration or another. Regardless, as we go through life, I believe we need perspective, balance, peace, and humor.

If you want but can't, it may mean you don't want it enough.

It's better to try and regret than regret not trying.

The deeper the pit you're falling into,
the more chance you have to learn how to fly.

If you don't care where you are, you'll never feel lost.

Beware. The light at the end of the tunnel may be an oncoming train.

A man is mature when he can smile
<u>for</u> the one who offended him.

"Time you enjoy wasting is not wasted time."
-- Marthe Troly-Curtin (1884 - ?)
From the novel, "Phrynette Married," 1912
(This line was re-quoted by John Lennon.)

Don't be nervous if someone is driving ahead of you. The world is round... just envision that you're driving first, and the other car is lagging far behind!

Shit happens. Hit flush and move on.

Life doesn't always turns out as we want, but as it should be.

1/7 of our lives are Mondays.

If a person really wants to live, medicine is helpless.

The Bimbo Has Brains

If you want girls to be running after you, become a bus driver.

There are two mysterious people, living in my house.
They are Somebody and Nobody.
Somebody did it, and Nobody knows who.

The most effective cleaning time is the 15 minutes between your friend's call and their arrival at your house.

Love helps to kill time. And time helps to kill love.

I'm not fat; I'm easier to see.

Nerve cells are born and die, but fat cells live forever!

You never realize what you have until it's gone… toilet paper, for example.

The poll results are in… the majority of people want an extra day between Saturday and Sunday.

The reason why I hate mornings so much is that they start while I'm still sleeping.

A human is afraid of two things: to live and to die.
We get used to most everything else gradually.

I do very bad things, and I do them extremely well.

The pleasures of life can be both innocent and guilty.

My blood type is high test coffee.

Team work is important; it helps put the blame on someone else.

*You work so you have money to live,
but because you work, you lack time to live.*

If no volunteers come forward, they get appointed.

People say nothing's impossible, but I do nothing every day.

Life Is Funny That Way

Laziness is when a person doesn't even fake that he's working.

A healthy sleep not only makes your life longer, but also shortens the workday.

*When we do something well the first time
no one appreciates how difficult it was.*

**A smart person thinks that he's like the rest of the people.
A stupid person thinks that everyone else is like him.**

In disagreement, truth is born. When conflict boils, truth evaporates.

You can't drown your sorrows; they can swim.

*When stressed, I like to eat ice cream, chocolate, and sweets.
This is because the word "stressed" spelled backwards is "desserts."*

If you think you are too small to make an impact, you've never slept in a dark room with a mosquito.

Sometimes, a true friend gives his paw, not his hand.

There are only seven days in the week, and "someday" isn't one of them.

Everyone has a friend who laughs funnier than he jokes.

"Sometimes good things fall apart, so better things can fall together."
-- Marilyn Monroe (1926 – 1962)
American actress

A friend is like a book. You don't need to read all of them. Just pick the best ones.

"Everything will be okay in the end. If it's not okay, it's not the end."
-- John Lennon (1940-1980)
English singer-songwriter-musician,
founding member of The Beatles

AFTERWORD

The Vile in Domestic Violence

For all the following data, I sincerely thank:
- National Coalition Against Domestic Violence (NCADV)
- United States Department of Justice
- National Intimate Partner and Sexual Violence Survey
- EVE (Ending Violence Everywhere) Foundation
- Department of Defense Family Advocacy Program

When it comes to your intimate partner, do you find yourself feeling fearful or concerned for your safety? Due to their actions, have you been injured, whether or not you sought treatment? Have you needed or contacted a crisis hotline, housing or legal services, or a victim's advocacy service? Due to the challenges of the relationship, have you missed at least one day of work or school?

Domestic abuse comes in many forms. Victims often suffer more than one type, ranging from emotional and psychological, to physical and sexual. The end result is the same. The victim changes behavior to try and please the abusive partner or to stay safe.
- In the U.S.A. nearly 20 people per minute are physically abused by the intimate partner… that's 10-million women and men in a single year.
- 20,000 phone calls ring in on a typical day to domestic violence hotlines.
- 19.3 million women and 5.1 million men have been stalked by their lovers.

Physical Violence

1 in 5 women and 1 in 7 men have been victims of severe physical violence to the point they feared or believed they or someone close to them would be harmed or killed. Severe physical violence by an intimate partner includes being hit with a fist or something hard, being beaten, getting pushed or pulled violently, or getting slammed against something.
- Intimate partner violence accounts for 15% of all violent crimes.
- 1 out of every 15 children are exposed to intimate partner violence every year, with 90% of them being eyewitnesses to the abuse.
- The presence of a gun in a domestic violence situation increases the risk of homicide by 500%.

The Vile in Domestic Violence

- Only 34% of people injured by intimate partners receive medical care for their injuries. Victims of intimate partner violence lose a total of 80 million days of paid work annually. The cost of this violence exceeds $8.3-billion per year.

Rape & Marital Rape

Nearly 1 in 10 women in the United States has been raped by an intimate partner. Only 36% of all rape victims ever report the crime to police. The percentage of married victims who report spousal rape is even lower. Marital rape is the most underreported form of sexual assault.

Until 1976, state laws specifically exempted spousal rape from general rape laws. In 1976, Nebraska became the first state to legally recognize nonconsensual intercourse with a spouse as rape. By 1993, all 50 states had either completely or partially repealed their spousal rape exemptions.

- Many Americans still do not believe that marital rape is actually rape.
- 18% of female victims of spousal rape say their children witnessed the crime.
- Between 10-14% of married women will be raped at some point during their marriages.
- Males make up the majority of perpetrators in sexual violence against both women and men. Perpetrators of non-sexual abuse against men are mostly women.

Psychological & Emotional Abuse

The presence of emotional abuse is the largest single risk factor and greatest predictor of physical violence, especially where a woman is called names to put her down or make her feel bad. Emotionally abusive partners also commit murder or murder-suicide. Women are most at risk of being killed when they leave their partners. Nearly half of all women and men in the United States have experienced psychological aggression by an intimate partner.

- Perpetrators use psychological abuse to traumatize their victims, along with verbal abuse, threats of acts, physical acts, and coercive tactics… all intended to control, terrorize, and denigrate.
- Emotional abuse is responsible for long-term problems with health, such as asthma, severe headaches, and diabetes, not to mention self-esteem, depression, and anxiety.
- Psychological abuse frequently occurs prior to or concurrently with physical or sexual abuse.

Indicators & Tactics

Does your partner:

- Threaten to harm you, your children or family, and/or your pets?
- Humiliate you?
- Tell you you're worthless, that no one else could ever love you?
- Isolate you from your friends and/or family?
- Tell you what you can and cannot do?
- Control or monitor your behavior and/or prevent you from having independent activities, such as work, community involvement, or taking educational classes?
- Withhold information from you?
- Undermine your confidence or sense of self-worth?
- Tell you that you are crazy?
- Demean you in public or in private?
- Act overly jealous or possessive and/or accuse you of having affairs if you even talk to another man?
- Constantly criticize your actions, size, appearance, and abilities?
- Make you feel you do nothing right?
- Blame you for everything that goes wrong?
- Stalk you?
- Threaten, intimidate, harass, or punish you if you don't comply with demands?
- Control or deny access to money or control what is spent and how it is spent?
- Cause you to feel guilt over things that are not your fault?
- Use the children to control you, by undermining your parental authority or threatening to separate you from them?

Survivors are frequently reluctant to disclose their victimization for various reasons, including shame, embarrassment, fear of retribution from their perpetrators, or fear they may not receive support from law enforcement.

Dial **9-1-1** if you are in danger!

For anonymous, confidential help 24/7, call the
National Domestic Violence Hotline at
1-800-799-SAFE (7233).

Go online to **www.DomesticShelters.org**
Or **www.TheHotline.org**

ABOUT THE AUTHOR

Cathy Burnham Martin's first published work was at age 6, when an early poem won a town library contest. That was back when her parents refused to let her have the then-popular Chatty Cathy doll, stating that one chatty Cathy in the house was more than enough.   Though poetry took a back seat, she has driven her writing and blabbing proficiencies along a highly eclectic career path through recruiting as Associate Director of Admissions, corporate communications as Director of Marketing for a telecommunications company, television broadcasting as News anchor with an ABC affiliate, management as Station Manager for an award-winning PEG access station, and bank organizing as Investor Relations Officer and Senior Vice President of Marketing. An active board member and volunteer, she received Easter Seals' David P. Goodwin Lifetime Commitment Award.

This professional voiceover artist, corporate communications geek, musical actress, journalist, and dedicated foodie earned numerous awards as a television news anchor and business woman. She has written, produced, and hosted groundbreaking documentaries, TV specials, and news reports, from the Moscow Super Power Summit and the opening of the Berlin Wall to coverage of New Hampshire's First-in-the-Nation Presidential Primaries.

A born storyteller, Cathy is a business speaker, a member of the Actors Equity Association, and a media coach. A Professional Member of the National Speakers Association since 1995, she has been dubbed "The Morale Booster" and continues speaking and coaching through SpeakEasy Corporate Communications.

Cathy Burnham Martin narrates her books as well as those of other authors. Audiobooks appear on such sites as Audible.com as well as from Amazon and iTunes. In addition to fiction and nonfiction books, Cathy writes articles for the **GoodLiving123.com** blog.